THE CATALYST

THE CATALYST
A Life Devoted To Others

by
Arthur Weider, Ph. D.

DORRANCE PUBLISHING CO., INC.
PITTSBURGH, PENNSYLVANIA 15222

Dedicated to my patients who collaborated with me
in attempting to prove the Talmudic dictum:

*...He who saves one soul
is likened to one who saves the entire universe...*

TABLE OF CONTENTS

PREFACE

In this volume, I hope to explore the dimensions and dynamisms of one kind of catalyst. The change agent in the behavioral sciences deals with the unconscious and conscious elements of clients or patients. The prism through which the following scripts are viewed, appraised, and sometimes altered are affected by the scientist and sometimes even changed as a consequence of the instrument. Thus, we don't see things as they are, but as we are, with different observers tending to view different behaviors differently.

For these and other reasons, it may be useful to know something about this observer, the author, through biographical and longitudinal psychohistorical perspectives detailing his own evolution into a professional clinical psychologist. Therefore, Chapter 1 is devoted to him as the first patient to come under scrutiny, with other patients following in successive chapters. The names of patients have been changed for obvious reasons.

Arthur Weider
New York City, 1994

Note: The names of individuals mentioned in privileged or confidential anecdotes have been changed to protect identities.

The author at 4 with his Father

The author "at sea" when 5

The author at 13 going through
with his "rites of passage"

The author as a graduate student at 21;
the pipe was never lit

The author with his mentor, Dr. David Wechsler
in his lab at Bellevue Psychiatric Hospital, 1941

Acknowledgments

The author gratefully acknowledges permission to quote Bob Dylan's lyric "The Times They Are A-Changing'," copyright © 1963, 1964 by Warner Bros. Music, copyright renewed 1991 by Special Rider Music. All rights reserved. International copyright secured. Reprinted by permission. The author also gratefully acknowledges permission to quote from "Operation Sidewinder," copyright © 1970, 1986 by Sam Shepard, from *The Unseen Hand and Other Plays* by Sam Shepard. Used by permission of Bantam Books, a division of Bantam Doubleday Dell Publishing Group, Inc.

PART I

MY PERSONAL LIFE

The South Bronx, before air conditioning, was an unusually warm borough, especially in the summer; so much so that relief was often sought on the fire escape, beside open windows, or by just sitting on one's front stoop. It was the latter that I often chose for my summer refuge. Too poor and too young even to qualify for the usual two-week fresh air sleep-away summer camp upstate, I took my place in front of my tenement with pad and pencil and Mickey Mouse watch in order to clock the numbered trolley cars as they passed to and fro on the East 169th Street line. This afforded me my free summer recreation of creative management.

The love of numbers on the trolleys, the time they passed going and the time they took to return, held a certain fascination for an eight-year-old in the summer of '28; I guess my respect for statistics evolved from this early hobby. Patience, another quality to stand me in good stead later on in life as a behavioral scientist, also developed at an early stage—at nine, to be exact.

A large milk company advertised in a print promotion to send a packet of ten envelopes with different flower seeds for ten cents. Early in June, I sent off my request and, a few weeks later, started my daily vigil early in the morning, waiting for the mailman to deliver my ten envelopes of seeds. Each morning during July, I would accost the mailman, to no avail. Late in August, my prayers were answered—my faith in patience, advertising, and horticulture were all confirmed simultaneously.

Meal times in my home were eventful occasions, full of exciting biplays among all the characters, especially between my brothers and me. Those with whom I have supped in past decades are sunk into their graves and my mind, but I shall never forget the many times that I would expectorate upon my food to ensure that it would be there upon my return to my place—if I were called away by my mother, a friend, or a biological urge of equal intensity. Frequently, the food was gone even after I took such great pains to have it saved!

Another example of brotherly love was in the sleeping arrangements necessary to accommodate me and my brothers, as we all had to share a bedroom with one bed. Thus, it was necessary for me to sleep between my two brothers and, to make more room in our bed, I slept next to each of their feet—that is, my older brother's feet were to my left and my middle brother's feet to my right. Talk about closeness!

THE CATALYST

During the fall of this same year, I remember my father showing my mother his neck, and the lump she felt moved her to agree that he should consult a physician. The latter suggested that the lump be watched. Some months later, a surgeon removed an undiagnosed cancer from my father's stomach and told my family (but not him) that he had six months to live. That was late December 1929—two months after the stock market crash and the beginning of the so-called Great Depression. This was to be a depression for us in every sense of the word.

I remember visiting my father one Friday afternoon, a few days after his surgery. He would always ask me: "Baby, how are you doing in school?"

"I'm doing fine. This morning I skipped from 5A to 5B, so that at the end of the term, I'll go into the sixth grade."

"You're a smart boy, Baby," was all he said, while his face grimaced in pain. He did not see me hold back my tears.

Days later, he came home and our house revolved around him and his needs. Our dining room became his bedroom, and we all took turns keeping him company and nursing him. In the early spring, my mother made ready for our Passover seder, which we all realized would be the last with our father at the head of the table—truly the last supper!

We had him dressed in his finest blue serge suit, and we all fought back tears all during our meal and services as I, the youngest, asked the traditional four questions. One by one, we excused ourselves to find a place to bawl our eyes out. While it was never mentioned among us—the family members—to ourselves, each vowed never to have a seder again. Indeed, I have never had the urge even to accept an invitation to attend one since.

We dreaded July, and late in the month, the 24th, to be exact, in the early evening, my father was failing fast. His weight had gone down in six months from 235 to eighty-five pounds. the minyan, or Jewish quorum of rabbis and elders, appeared in their black garb and surrounded his bed, chanting their prayers for the terminally ill and dying. My mother and older sisters were in the living room in the front of our railroad flat, ranting and wailing as a young widow and three daughters deserve to do. My two older brothers were elsewhere in the apartment, but I know—at ten years of age—that this was a momentous event in my life with my father and that I did not want to miss even a minute away from him. Indeed, I wanted to be with him at his side until he gasped his last breath. Curiously, none of my family inquired about the youngest child—where he was during this traumatic episode that would alter our relationship forever.

In the meantime, I witnessed one of the little old men take the white bed sheet and move it ever so slowly over my father's drawn, breathless, lifeless face. During this moment that I knew would live forever in my heart and memory, I was aware that my father would not only not attend my bar mitzvah and my graduations from high school and college, but I vowed that all of my children's names would begin with the letter, "J," for Joseph, his name. (The usual tradition is to name a newborn child after a recently deceased parent or grandparent.)

After the week of shiva, the initial mourning period, the month of August marked the beginning of the period of official, religious mourning which would last for one entire year. What it meant for a son was attendance at the local synagogue in the early morning prior to school, twice in the late afternoon, and early in the evening. The Kaddish was recited at each occasion and, when away from home and the local synagogue, one would have to search out a synagogue closest to friends or relatives and the Kaddish was recited there.

After one year of these observances, one could again listen to radio music or recordings or go to the movies, as the official period of mourning ended. The only remaining requirement was that, on holy days and the yearly anniversary, the departed would be remembered at Yiskor services with the memorial chant. I, however, due to some precocious obsession, or perhaps out of sheer devotion, have never since lain down to sleep at night without including the Yiskor in my prayers. During this period of my life, I became aware that I would have to overcome adversity by myself and that I could not depend on a father to guide and counsel me through life's vicissitudes.

During that August, another event occurred which was responsible for shaping an aspect of my personality. As is the custom in Greek, Italian, and Jewish households where tragedy strikes, exodus is made to the seashore for its recuperative effects upon the body and spirit. Although our month was spent at Coney Island among concerned and loving relatives, I bitterly missed my father, who used to take me into the ocean and ride the waves. Late afternoons were spent along on the boardwalk paying Skee Ball at a local gaming parlor. It was there that I first learned about psychokinesis—but, of course, I learned the term and concept decades later. This occurred fortuitously, as so many insights into the self do.

For days, I had approached the concentric circles of Skee Ball with trepidation, but also with a sense of challenge. Each afternoon, I paid for the six bocce balls and threw them willy nilly toward the circles, hoping some would get into the small circle, but none did. One day, I threw a ball and, lo and behold, it went into the small circle. I stopped, thought, and tried to replicate (the word I used then was "reproduce") the same movement of my left arm and hand, and the motion, and breathing. Sure enough, I succeeded again, and again, and again. Eureka! I could control the movement of my arm; my mind could control my arm. On many of the remaining days, I collected enough coupons to earn a cuckoo clock and a kewpie doll, both of which are long gone. But the lesson of psychokinesis has given me much self-confidence and supported the adage: "What the mind can conceive, man or (boy), can achieve!"

THE CATALYST

The remaining years were full of depression—emotional and economic—in our household. The anxieties and insecurities my mother brought with her as an immigrant child at the age of sixteen were rehearsed daily and, unwittingly, we introjected these into our own psyches. An episode I have never forgotten, unfortunately, or perhaps not unfortunately, as it helped me to learn how to overcome adversity throughout my personal as well as my professional life, concerned a pair of shoes...sneakers, to be exact.

One Saturday evening, I announced to my mother that I would need a pair of sneakers for the coming Monday's P.T. (Physical Training, as it was known in 1930 junior high school).

"Nicht do keine gelt," was all she said.

I pleaded with: "But, Mamma, I can't go to school without them and I don't want to miss my class in P.T."

She countered with: "Next week, I'll have the money."

I said, "But, Mamma, if you'll have it next week, you must have it now. Besides, I will have them for an additional week earlier when I need them." The sum of money involved was a big $2.25, I remember.

My argument must have worked, because we went to the corner shoe store of Mr. Dopkin—I even recall his name—and got the Keds sneakers. Approximately twenty-five years later, after my mother passed away, I remembered this episode when searching through her bedroom closet. We came upon her bank books and about $45,000 in cash; hidden for a rainy day, I guess. I wondered if she had had a little cache when she told me, "There's no money," for my sneakers that Saturday evening.

This always reminded me of a very popular television series which I know my mother watched as did many other millions: "I remember Mama." In these skits, the mother led her daughters to believe that she had funds for their dowries or education, even though her closet was bare. The knowledge that she had a cache gave them a sense of security. My mother, on the other hand, apparently had the cache, but rather than tell us and thereby give us a sense of security, she kept this from us, thereby instilling even more of a sense of insecurity.

As a consequence of these events, I vowed never to instill a sense of insecurity and anxiety in any loved one for whom I was ever responsible; indeed, I usually gave the impression of prosperity and optimism even when funds were actually low. As a matter of fact, whenever I was asked for a certain amount of money, I would usually double the amount asked for and give a little extra for security!

At twelve, I began to work after school in order to have my own petty cash which I used for carfare to high school, and occasionally lunch or a movie. My mother usually prepared my lunch, which each semester consisted of the same menu; that is, I could always know that a swiss cheese sandwich was in the brown bag for the fall and an egg sandwich for the next entire spring semester. To this day, I wonder why I never told my mother to vary my diet and give me a choice of other foods.

From the age of eight, I considered myself a music lover, especially of the classics. Even at that age, I could recognize all of the nine symphonies of Beethoven, the four symphonies of Brahms, and the six symphonies of Tchaikovsky. As I got older, I found Mozart easy to absorb and would win approving glances when I would call out the composer and the number of the symphony. Concertos came later.

I recall this fact in this context, as a conflict usually arose with my older brother—older by six years. His interests were in the New York Yankees, and we would frequently go to double-headers, taking along several sandwiches for each of us and sitting in the bleachers for twenty-five cents, watching four or five hours of baseball. On several occasions, when I had decided not to go because I preferred to listen to the Sunday afternoon radio concerts of the New York Philharmonic, he became so angry as to inflict on me specifically on my mother's general instruction to save the cost of electricity. He would go down to the basement and take the fuse out so that I could not listen to the concert, and we would save the two or three hours of electricity. I, of course, was too young and scared to go down to the basement alone. In time, I found enough courage to venture down to the fuse box and gained the confidence to overcome this type of adversity, also. Although, like many other children of the Depression, I am still acutely aware of lights carelessly left burning, my love of classical music has flourished.

At fourteen, June 6, 1933, to be precise—and I want to be precise about this date since it bears such significance for me professionally—I discovered a book on our kitchen table which determined the course of my career. Our kitchen doubled as a library, study hall, sitting and living room, as well as eatery. I remember the date, as it was the last day of my oldest brother's semester at CCNY, and he brought home *Elements of Human Psychology* by Howard C. Warren and Leonard Carmichael, and left it on the kitchen table. I found it and began reading it. I read it thoroughly that summer and compulsively underlined parts of the text, apparently with a ruler. I have cherished this book for almost sixty years as an inspiration, and attribute to it the fateful role of guidance counselor I never had nor really ever needed in any person. I have come to feel that the book discovered me as much as I discovered the book. I do believe that things of this sort are possible, but just how, I leave to others to fathom. I will go into some detail about the senior author of this textbook, when some dozen years later into my career, another inexplicable coincidence occurred.

When, in my fourteenth years, I announced to my mother that I had decided upon a career as a psychologist, she exclaimed: "Oy vey, a Kishef

Macher!" in her shrill, low-German Yiddish. This was the name for a maker of magic, a shady sort of hocus-pocus character. One sees she wasn't too far off the mark about sixty years go in her understanding of psychology as a science or an art. As a matter of fact, psychology was still a part of the department of Philosophy and Psychology in many of the major universities, and Clinical Psychology as a discipline was still in its infancy. It is small wonder that an immigrant lady in the South Bronx had not yet heard of psychology as a career.

A few years later, I graduated from high school, and I remember with dismay when I visited my English teacher for the last time and was asked what career had I chosen. I replied I was planning to become a psychologist, and he tried to discourage me, as I would have to obtain a doctorate. I recall returning to the same high school some years later, seeing the same English teacher, and reporting to him that I had just obtained my doctorate. He did not appear to be impressed. A few weeks after orientation of new students at New York University, I arranged to take a battery of placement and aptitude tests. I must have done well, as I was not placed in any remedial or prerequisite courses and was advised by one of the assistant professors in the Psychology Department to consider Engineering, as I had "aced" the Minnesota Paper Form Test in fifteen minutes instead of the allotted twenty. "No, thank you, Professor Madden; I plan to major in Psychology, not Engineering."

Ten years later, when I was leaving New York City to accept a teaching post as associate professor of Medical Psychology in the Department of Psychiatry and Mental Hygiene at the University of Louisville School of Medicine in Louisville, Kentucky, I stopped by to see my colleague, Professor Madden (who was still assistant professor, I might add). He recalled how I had decided on Psychology rather than Engineering. "The two disciplines are somewhat related," he suggested.

In order to afford tuition at NYU, which I chose because I wanted to assist Dr. David Wechsler, whom I had read about in various journals, and I knew he was not only one of the few professors of Medical Psychology in New York City, or in the United States, for that matter, but that he was also at Bellevue Psychiatric Hospital. It took real chutzpah for a poor kid from the South Bronx, practically an orphan and long before the student loan days or GI Bill of Rights, Pell, and New York State scholarship programs to look forward to a private university because of one professor. Although I was only seventeen, I was thinking ahead to my masters and doctorate degrees in a way which now reminds me of my experience at my father's bedside, as a I projected myself into the future as a parent, vowing to name all of my progeny with a "J"...which has come to pass.

In order to make ends meet, I worked after college classes as a copy boy at the *New York World-Telegram and Sun* for $15 per week. I had to join the only union I ever joined, but happily did so, as Heywood Broun, the eminent journalist, was founder and president of the Newspaper Guild of America, still a very prestigious and venerable union. I also worked twenty hours per week between classes, on weekends, and during summers and holidays for fifty cents an hour under the National Youth Administration (NYA) program—part of President Franklin Delano Roosevelt's answer to the Great Economic Depression to help college students.

For three years, day in and day out, during academic semesters, summer vacations, holidays, and religious holy days, our white, black, gray, and brown Norwegian bred rats had to be fed, starved, and readied for experiments in learning and the effects of centrifugal force. After the rats had learned a particular maze, some of the walls would be changed and the rats would have to learn increasingly difficult and complex paths through the maze.

Other experiments utilized the Lashley jumping apparatus, which consisted of large, white, screen-like board placed about fifteen to twenty feet from a high stool upon which the hungry rat was placed. A blast of air forced the rat to make a choice of jumping to one of two doors cut out on the white screen in front. One door had a triangle on it and was placed either to the right or to the left. At no time did this hinged door open, so that a rat choosing this door would fall upon the apron in front of the screen. If the circle was chosen, that door would open upon a stash of food pellets behind. The finer discriminations which had to be made between the circle and an ellipse were exceedingly stressful for the rat, which would stand on its hind legs, defecate, urinate, hesitate, fall to the ground in epileptic-like tonic and clonic contractions, and demonstrate other experimental neurotic-like symptoms. The year we hesitated to name these behaviors "experimental neurosis," a group of experimental psychologists form the University of Michigan's Department of Psychology, who were on their way to the American Association for the Advancement of Science, showed us a film entitled "Experimental Neurosis in Animal Behavior," which portrayed much the same behaviors we elicited in our rats. This group won the $1,000 prize for the most original and creative experimentation.

I live by the maxim: "I need my children as much as they need me; I need my students as much as they need me; I need my patients as much as they need me," and I needed those rats, then, as much as they needed me. An integral part of my career, education, training, and experience was predicated upon the discipline that those creatures instilled in me. Through them I learned the simple truism, "Never put off for tomorrow what needs to be done today." It was my responsibility as a lab assistant to two young professors to come to the lab and look after these hungry rats; to keep their cages clean, to see that they were watered, to see that they were fed if they were part of the control group, and to put them through their learning schedules if they were part of the experimental group. They helped to instill in me an experimental bias which I found essential to the pursuit of a clinical psychological career with students, clients, and patients.

Another event which had long-lasting repercussions occurred one evening during my junior year of college. It was getting late and I could have gone home to the Bronx for my dinner, but I was eager to stay and study in the college library where it was not only quiet and conducive to study but the journals were available for researching the articles I needed to write a paper. I put my hand into my pocket and found a single nickel; with it I could either get home on the subway or use it to buy dinner. I opted to eat and worry about getting home later. I went to the local Automat on lower Broadway and Eighth Street, put the nickel in the slot, and obtained a glass of milk which I nursed for several minutes before returning to the library and getting in several more hours of work on my paper. When it came time to go home, I walked to the subway at Astor Place. I had seen many riders sneak under the turnstiles, but I never thought I could ever do this myself. Some years earlier, I had heard some wag say: "Rules are made for intelligent people to break, sometimes." I must have felt that this was as good a time as any to break a rule. Hesitating before the uptown turnstiles, I saw that no one was noticing me and bent down under the turnstile when I saw the train approach, committing my first crime; I flew into the train and felt my heart pound for minutes until I arrived at Fourteenth Street and changed for the uptown express. Needless to say, I could not sleep that night, but tossed and turned with guilt and could not speak a word of this event to anyone, not until almost twenty years later when I was in my didactic personal analysis. I could not wait until the next day when I returned to the scene of the crime, approached the clerk in that same change booth—not token booth, as these were the days before tokens—and handed over a nickel to the startled clerk who asked, "What's this for?"

"Yesterday, I sneaked in without paying my nickel by going under the turnstile," I said haltingly.

"Forget it," was all he said, and I disappeared.

Case closed? Not really. This brought to mind a conversation I once had with my father many years earlier. It should be remembered that I had very few conversations alone with my father, but this was one of those precious moments which I had filed away in my memory bank. It was related to money, and thus was relevant to the nickel episode and almost every other time I put my hand into my pockets for change or bills. My father said, "Baby, never count how much money you have with you; if you have to count, you'll never have enough. You should be in such good shape that you'll not have to know how much you have!" And so it has been down through the years; I have never really counted how much money I have had with me, either change or bills. Actually, I have always had enough!

THE CATALYST

During those solitary years of running rats through mazes, music was my solace, and the psych lab reverberated with Tchaikovsky, especially his Symphony Number Six, the "Pathetique," and the bombastic Number Five. We may have hesitated at the anthropomorphic error of labeling our rats' behavior as experimental neurosis, but we were certain that they were exposed to the finest in classical music. The "we" referred to above consisted of the principal investigator of our projects, Dr. Theodore C. Schneirla, professor of Comparative Animal Psychology, Herman A. Witkin, graduate student soon to receive his doctorate, and myself. We were conscientious, diligent, and devoted to our research and our rats. One or the other always accompanied me in the lab to observe the rats' learning behavior.

Indulging my love for music, I would sometimes go to student rushes at Carnegie Hall on weekend evenings, or else to Lewisohn Stadium on the campus of City College where, for twenty-five cents, I could hear the New York Philharmonic on a summer night. I recall especially one evening devoted to the annual George Gershwin concert, listening to his "Rhapsody in Blue" under the stars of this magnificent Romanesque amphitheater, and on another occasion sitting in a light drizzle and listening spellbound to Beethoven's Symphony Number Nine, "The Chorale," with its "Ode to Joy." On another evening, I was moved to a memorable high when I heard the sixteen-year-old Lorin Hollander majestically play the Beethoven Piano Concerto Number Five, "The Emperor."

I was in my late teens, and I was one of a small group of college seniors who knew that we must apply to graduate school. I attended staff conferences at Bellevue Psychiatric Hospital on Friday evenings, much as people went to the movies for entertainment, except I learned much about psychopathology and mental illness from the actual case material that was presented there. I heard of exceptional cases and current literature that was recommended to the psychiatric residents, and I would avail myself of the library facilities. I would also attend conferences throughout the city at the Academy of Medicine, the Academy of Sciences, and the Mount Sinai Hospital, the Post-Graduate Hospital, and the Payne Whitney Psychiatric Clinic. I rarely spent any money for so-called entertainment, first of all, because I had none to spend, and secondly, because I found these conferences more rewarding and they were free. Emotionally and privately, these were the halcyon days of my life. I was deeply immersed in the scientific study of Psychology, I was participating in important animal research in learning, I was developing an undying love for classical music, and I was preparing for a career that would bring me confidence, insight, and security. In February 1940, it occurred to me, and to me alone, as I still had not found a mentor or even a college counselor who would guide me in my quest toward a career even though I knew I was preparing to become a psychologist, that, as I would be graduating in June, perhaps I could get a job, even at a state hospital, simply for the experience. Consequently, I took myself to the medical library of neighboring St. Vincent's Hospital and scoured the Directory of State Hospitals for the names and addresses of the superintendents listed for New York State, Connecticut, New Jersey, and Pennsylvania institutions. I framed a letter requesting a job in almost any capacity, stating that I would be a recent college graduate with a major in Psychology, and that I hoped to obtain a masters degree and a doctorate, eventually.

I recall that I was rather secretive about this venture, not telling any of my college friends who were also majoring in Psychology and who would also be graduating with me. This was a good idea for me alone. I sent 300 letters, which I typed one at a time to each superintendent, and once again found myself waiting patiently for the mail to arrive. Among the half-dozen replies I received was one from Dr. Woodman at the Middletown State Hospital, Middletown, New York, inviting me to join his staff as psychiatric aide, as no line existed for psychologists, but in actuality, I would be the psychological intern at fifty-seven dollars per month, and receive room and board. Could I come the seventy miles for an interview? I was there within the week, and we decided that I should begin May 1, which meant I would miss my graduation. My official duties were vague, but I put together a program for my internship that consisted of the following: I would attend staff meetings each morning; I would teach a course to the student nurses in Psychology, Anthropology, and Sociology; I would administer neuropsychodiagnostic tests to patients using both objective and the newer projective techniques; and I would do research.

Originally, I had decided to attend NYU because Dr. David Wechsler was professor of Medical Psychology and also on the staff of Bellevue Psychiatric Hospital. During my last year, I had enrolled in his course on psychopathology and took it during both semesters. This not only gave me an opportunity to make myself known to him, but I became thoroughly familiar with his newly standardized army intelligence test, which was then known as the Wechsler-Bellevue Adult Intelligence Test. I volunteered to work for him, and he arranged for me to attend staff conferences on Friday evenings where psychiatrists presented inpatients who presented difficult diagnostic problems. These were not only exceedingly well-researched and evaluated, but they were informative. I met some of the most eminent and published psychiatrists in the New York City area, many of whom were refugees from Hitler's Europe. Eminent psychiatrists and psychoanalysts like Sandor Rado, Franz Alexander, Paul Schilder, and David Rappaport gave seminars and made presentations. The case studies, bibliographic references, and additional readings they urged were so rewarding and encouraging that I knew I was on my way and that my career was beginning to take shape.

As the Stanford-Binet had been standardized on fewer than twenty adults but had been administered for years to adults as well as children and was really the only individually administered intelligence test available, it occurred to me to take the recently developed Wechsler-Bellevue Scale to Middletown State Hospital. I had my research project: I would administer both the Binet and the Wechsler to the same adult patients and see what relationships were found; e.g. correlations and clinically valid findings. Furthermore, as I was planning to go to Columbia University for my masters degree, this study could fulfill the requirements for a masters dissertation, which I might even be able to publish in a psychological journal.

My association with Dr. Wechsler became close and warm, and I felt I had finally found the mentor I had dreamed about a half-dozen years before. When I told him I would be a psych intern at Middletown and that I was going to do a comparative study of the Binet and his adult intelligence scale, he was delighted. He sent me off with his blessings and best wishes. From then on, and for the next four decades, we were close associates, published together, and were warm friends, which ended with his death.

In preparation for my new status as a member of a psychiatric staff, and to add years and dignity to my youthful face of twenty, I began to grow a mustache. As a matter of fact, on my personnel form at the hospital I stated my age as twenty-one, as that was a requirement to receive a state salary. I also let it be known to a senior psychiatrist, Dr. Bernard Zugar, who was in charge of my supervision, that I had already graduated from college. Much to my chagrin, some weeks later, he pointed out to me that my name was listed in the *New York Times* as having graduated that June and I had to confess to him my real age. We became fast friends and real colleagues, as I learned much about inpatient psychiatry, diagnosis, insulin and electric shock therapy, and state hospital administration from him. He also taught me a bit about the New York Stock Exchange and which stocks to buy—at least which stocks he would buy. He also taught me a lot about tennis and Chinese food.

I embarked upon a routine full of learning: breakfast at 8 A.M.; staff conference and presentations of three patients from 8:30 until 10:00; psychological assessment of inpatients until 12:00; lunch until 1:00; lectures to nursing students until 2:00. This was followed by research, wherein I administered the Binet to those patients who had been tested with the Wechsler. On occasion, I would test another inpatient who would be conferenced shortly. Dinner was at 5:00; and I was on the tennis courts by 6:00. This was the life! By September 1940, I was ready to return to New York City with about thirty-five cases of adults who had been given complete Binets and Wechslers, and I enrolled at Columbia University for my masters degree in Psychology. I arranged to volunteer at Dr. Wechsler's lab at Bellevue. I returned to the *World-Telegram and Sun* and worked evenings and weekend and I worked in the Animal Comparative Psychology Lab at Columbia. I spent most of my days in classes at Columbia or at the Neurological Institute or at the Psychiatric Institute. The latter two institutions were in upper Manhattan and were associated with Columbia University Medical Center.

My entertainment consisted of attending staff conferences Friday evenings at Bellevue, attending Grand Rounds at the Psychiatric Institute Thursday afternoons, reading for my courses, attending Psychiatric and Psychoanalytic Association Meetings at the New York Academy of Medicine at Fifth Avenue and 103rd Street, on various evenings, or listening to the New York Philharmonic Sunday afternoon concerts, which were broadcast live on radio. I soon learned how to study on the subways and became accustomed to background noises as a necessary cognitive dissonance variable to learning. Consequently, I could read or even study effectively while listening to Brahms, Berlioz, or Beethoven, and my recognition of the classics burgeoned from Albinoni to Vivaldi. To this day, background music facilitates all other intellectual activities that impinge on my sensorium, so I find that I can work at the computer, listen to classical music, and watch one or two television monitors, all at the same time.

One of my professors at the Psychiatric Institute, Dr. Joseph Zubin, upon hearing that I was interested in a comparative study of the Binet with the Wechsler, suggested that I get in touch with Dr. Arthur Benton at CCNY, who had recently obtained his Ph.D. at Columbia and was also collecting data on these two intelligence tests. I wasted not a moment, and visited Dr. Benton at his apartment near Fort Tryon Park and The Cloisters. We were both amazed that we had similar ideas for these two procedures and decided to pool our data together with that of Jean Blauvelt, a recent Columbia masters student. I wrote up the results and discussion for my masters dissertation, and we set up a table of "equivalent scores" for the Binet and the Wechsler, based on the regression equations derived from the correlation between the two tests. Thus, it was possible to predict the Wechsler IQ score from the Binet IQ score by referring to the table we published in October 1941 in *The Psychiatric Quarterly*; this was my first publication! I was twenty-two.

In the meantime, I began to think about getting a job in clinical psychology, and heard that the Eastern Psychological Association would be meeting on the new Brooklyn College campus. I noticed that a Dr. Albert Rabin was delivering a paper on the Wechsler. I attended, introduced myself, and told him of my association with Dr. Wechsler and my masters topic and pending publication, and wondered if he might have a job for me with a small stipend. He thought a few moments and then offered me a supervised internship as one of his assistants in the Psychology Department of the New Hampshire State Hospital, in Concord, New Hampshire. I would examine psychiatric patients with a battery of neuropsychodiagnostic tests, including projective techniques. I would obtain complete maintenance, including my own suite and $115 per month. I was ecstatic. This was the middle of April 1941, and once again, my mother attended a graduation which I had to miss; this one was for my masters degree at Columbia early in June.

I remember that I began to feel like a true professional, as I was getting paid and I was listed on the staff roster as "psychologist." I learned something every day from the psychiatric staff, the nursing students, the psychological staff, and the patients; from my very first encounter on the very first day with Sarah, a Protestant lady in her seventies who was diagnosed as a hebraphile paranoiac. She was sitting in a rocking chair on the porch of a building which I had to pass on my way to my meals. In passing, I smiled and went on my way. Later that afternoon, I went to pick up my mail and found a most beautiful hand-painted pansy which Sarah had made, and on the back, a message was written in the most compulsive fashion I ever saw. The message was a thank-you note for me for having smiled at her and how she would love to make my acquaintance.

Each succeeding morning, on my way to breakfast, there was Sarah, rocking in her chair and waiting for my smile. Finally, one day I chatted with her, and she handed me another beautifully hand-painted water color of a flower. A few weeks later, I read her hospital record and discovered that she was a native Yankee artist from Vermont, had taught art at Pratt Institute in Brooklyn, and lived in Greenwich Village. She had met a man who was an alcoholic, but married him "to save him." Life with him was hard, and she began to show signs of mental illness. She had to leave her job, and was hospitalized at The Brattleboro Retreat in Vermont, a private psychiatric institution, but as her funds were depleted, she was hospitalized at the New Hampshire State Hospital for many years, and what funds she had in trust were relegated to that institution so that she could be treated for life, if necessary.

During the course of her illness, she formulated a theory of religion wherein Hebrews had all the right answers about God, life on earth, and life in the hereafter; the one true religion! Indeed, Sarah had shelves upon shelves of books and manuscripts from rabbis and Talmudic scholars from all over our country who were carrying on a prolonged, philosophical correspondence with "Sarah C." at 105 Pleasant Street, Concord, New Hampshire; none realizing that the address was that of a mental hospital. Although we became friendly and I visited with her in her room from time to time, I was keenly aware of her abnormal preoccupation with Jews and

Hebrew lore, almost to the exclusion of all else in her life. This obsessiveness, along with her compulsive handwriting and early aggressive violent outbursts and illogical ideation system based upon an erroneous premise, as a syndrome, supported the diagnosis of paranoia. I learned much from Sarah, and she rewarded me with more than ten lovely, hand-painted water colors of flowers, which are framed as miniatures and are still hanging on my wall, more than fifty years later.

The peaceful, tranquil, bucolic surroundings of the hospital and environs that summer in New Hampshire will stay with me forever. I learned daily, not only about psychology and psychiatry, but about humanity and perspicacity. My evenings were devoted to listening to classical music from the Boston equivalent of WQXR, and to the Boston Symphony Orchestra from Tanglewood, as I sat with a calculator computing by hand ninety-two coefficient correlations, which took months to complete. True, a footnote to an article published by Dr. Rabin acknowledges this fact, and I learned much more about the Wechsler, so that a short form of this test became part of the psychologist's armamentarium and is still referred to in the field and literature.

In October 1941, I returned to New York City from New Hampshire by way of Northwestern University, where the American Psychological Association held its convention. I immediately arranged to study for my doctorate at NYU, and visited Dr. Wechsler at Bellevue. I told him I wanted to work *with* him, and not necessarily *for* him, on his staff.

Dr. Wechsler was the chief psychologist at Bellevue Psychiatric Hospital and professor of Medical Psychology at New York University. He was engaged in supervising more than fifteen clinical psychologists who were paid by the City of New York, Department of Hospitals, five interns, and two research psychologists on grants. He was also doing research of his own on psychogalvanic responses in emotionally charged situations, intelligence testing, and personality questionnaire construction.

He informed me that I would assist him in his own research and not be supervised by him as a member of his staff. I was fortunate, as he invited me to assist him in projects that he was working on at this time and arranged to offer me twenty-five dollars per week from his research budget. By now, I was being quoted in the literature on the Wechsler Adult Intelligence Scale and I had become proficient as a researcher, and he had confidence in my judgment and expertise. I enrolled for the doctorate at NYU, but took courses at the Psychiatric Institute and at Bellevue. I was attending conferences and staff meetings all over New York City at various hospitals in the evenings, and making contacts with some of the most renowned psychoanalysts and psychiatrists who had come to our shores as refugees from Hitler. Through Dr. Wechsler, I met eminent colleagues and attending meetings of his department, as well as meetings of the Psychiatric

Department. I had all the privileges of being on the Bellevue Psychiatric staff, and interacted with psychiatric residents and interns while being supervised by Dr. Wechsler and learning directly from him, at his side...in the real clinical fashion.

On December 7, 1941, between about 3:00 and 5:30, I was in the balcony of a Broadway theater and, upon leaving, I learned from a newspaper hawker in front of the Astor Hotel that the Japanese had bombed Pearl Harbor! My life and the lives of many Americans, indeed, the lives of people around the world, would be changed and never be the same again.

The following day, I was at the courthouse known as the Tombs, where prisoners awaiting arraignment before a judge are housed in lower Manhattan, near Chinatown. I was collecting data for a research project with Dr. Wechsler and examining prisoners on a test battery which could be used by judges and assistant district attorneys. This being Monday, a few of us went to a Chinese restaurant for lunch, but it was interrupted by the radio address of President Franklin D. Roosevelt, in which he spoke the words which history will remember always: "Yesterday, a day that will live in infamy, the Japanese bombed Pearl Harbor..."

Lives changed swiftly from that day forward. Research priorities and career paths were altered overnight. Indeed, World War II was to provide clinical psychology with a baptism of fire. All of psychology was going to be mobilized!

For us at Bellevue, 1942 ushered in momentous opportunities for research mandated by our government, now at war. The Wechsler-Bellevue Adult Intelligence Scale was to undergo a new standardization, as requested by the United States Army, and there was a pressing need for a quick screening instrument to reject neuropsychiatrically disturbed selectees at induction stations.

I continued with Dr. Wechsler at Bellevue, learning—in the truest sense—at my mentor's elbow. I became his leg man and gopher; traveled the East; went to Washington; spent much time in libraries; sought out executive, superior types of personnel in corporations, the military, and the New York Police Department. The Metropolitan Life Insurance Company and Continental Can Company cooperated with us and allowed us to test many of their supervisors in the standardization of an adult intelligence test. Officers in the armed services, as well as detectives and lieutenants of the NYPD, were also tested in our sample. I also had to find time to attend graduate classes and take examinations.

It has been said: "If you want to get something done, find a busy man (or woman) to do it!" I could not have been any busier during that fateful year of 1942, when Dr. Wechsler came to my office one afternoon and asked if I would like to go to the New York Hospital-Cornell University Medical Center and work with Dr. Harold G. Wolff. Two of my questions were:

"Where is the New York Hospital?" and "What about my research with him?" He informed me that the hospital was at East Sixty-Eighth Street, and that he would be our consultant and attend weekly meetings.

I mounted the stairs of the Third Avenue EL early one morning for one of the most significant interviews of my young life—to meet with the principal investigator of an interdisciplinary research team consisting of Dr. Harold G. Wolff, professor of Medicine, Psychiatry, and Neurology of the Cornell University Medical College; Dr. Bela Mittelmann, training psychoanalyst; and Dr. David Wechsler, psychological consultant. When the interview had ended, I was appointed research associate with an appointment at the Cornell University Medical College-New York Hospital.

Although I was the junior-ranking member of this illustrious team, I was assigned senior authorship of an extremely important article published in the *Journal of The American Medical Association,* 124:224, 1944: "The Cornell Selectee Index: A Method of Quick Testing of Selectees for the Armed Forces." I was responsible for aiding in the development of this comprehensive neuropsychiatric and psychosomatic questionnaire. I gathered data among "normal" populations and "neurotic and dysfunctional" patients. I assisted in the standardization, item analysis, tetrachoric correlations, coefficients of correlations for reliability and validity, and did much of the original writing for publication. A tetrachoric correlation is one in which numerical test scores are related to a diagnostic entity, rather than compared to another numerical test score. This brief screening test was administered to more than fifteen million male and female selectees in World War II. Requests for reprints came in from all over the country and armed forces at home and abroad. Indeed, we received requests from all over the world. Many universities, clinics and hospitals, department stores, city, state, and federal agencies, as well as corporations, were interested in the quick screening properties and scientific soundness of this instrument.

One letter came from Dr. Harold Vonachen, medical director of the Caterpillar Tractor Company, Peoria, Illinois, suggesting a Cornell-Caterpillar research program for mental health in industry; he was president of the American Association of Industrial Physicians and Surgeons, and invited Dr. Mittlemann and me to visit him. A grant was accepted, and we made bimonthly visits there, interviewed supervisory and executive staff in manufacturing, marketing, and industrial relations. Medical, psychosomatic, and borderline states were diagnosed as they impacted on job performance. Several articles appeared in the literature: *Psychosomatic Medicine, Transactions American Neurological Association,* and *Journal of Orthopsychiatric Association.* Our team also published in *War Psychiatry* and *Industrial Medicine,* and we were pioneers in human relations in industry back in 1944. Dr. Vonachen offered me a position as personnel consultant in his medical division, which I had to decline because I had been assigned to Cornell University Medical College to conduct military research for the armed forces for the duration.

I had visited army, navy, and submarine bases, including military hospitals, surgical, medical, and psychiatric wards as well as induction stations, throughout the country. I also went to the naval induction station on Whitehall Street to enlist as an ensign in 1944, but was told that Cornell Medical and the Committee for Medical Research, National Research Council, and the Office of Scientific Research and Development—the government agency funding our research—would not release me to the Department of the Navy.

The military installations I visited to test personnel consisted of many makeshift quonset huts and dozens of one- and two-story wooden buildings. In the summer, the heat was oppressive and, in the winter, the cold was depressive. As I had security clearance, I was given sleeping quarters in the officers' barracks and allowed to take my meals in the mess hall. All accommodations were spare and spartan. The soldiers, sailors, airmen, and marines were all cooperative and understood the purpose of our research. On several occasions, I had to test the students at Harvard Medical School, Yale Medical School, and Columbia Physicians and Surgeons, and there, too, the subjects were quick to realize the nature and worth of our test and research.

Research on many fronts continued, and Dr. Mittelmann and I made numerous trips to Caterpillar. In May 1945, Dr. Vonachen suggested that I spend my vacation in August at the plant, and use his spacious office while he was away on vacation, in order to "get the feel" of industrial psychology first-hand. I accepted his offer, arrived in Peoria, and checked into the grand, old, venerable Pere Marquette Hotel. Before he left, Dr. Vonachen once again offered me the job in his department. To put him off, I said: "When the war ends, I'll be at liberty to join you." Neither of us dreamed that, in the middle of August, the war would end! "I will try for January 1, 1946." After writing my report for Dr. Vonachen on my observations at Caterpillar, and knowing that wartime research at Cornell Medical would terminate, I really felt I could be ready to start January 1, 1946.

I was busy writing my doctoral dissertation and typing the manuscript myself, entrusting this labor of love to no one. I finished it in 1945. My course requirements were over, and I defended my thesis in April 1946. It was published: "Screening the Neuropsychiatrically Unfit Selectee From the Armed Forces," in December 1945. Once again, I was not able to attend a graduation, not even for the Ph.D., as I was in Peoria, Illinois, already working as the personnel consultant, with duties, responsibilities, students, and clients. While at Caterpillar, I was invited to join the graduate faculty of the Department of Psychology at Bradley University to teach several courses.

Another invitation came from the University of Illinois, Department of Psychology, for me to conduct a colloquium before the faculty and students for a weekend. Coincidentally, after being introduced before my presentation, I was compelled to inform the audience that, had it not been for the chairman, who had just called me to the lectern, I would not have become a psychologist, as he had authored the book I had read in the South Bronx during that summer a dozen years earlier. The chairman was Dr. Warren, who had co-authored *Elements of Human Psychology* in 1930. I gave my series of lectures on clinical psychology, test construction, the Cornell Index, psychosomatic medicine, and mental hygiene in industry. My slide presentations were effective, as was the material I had brought along to field any questions that might be put to me. I left Champaign-Urbana feeling good about myself, my presentation, and how far I had progressed professionally in a dozen years.

I attacked my duties at Caterpillar with great zeal, setting up an eight-pronged program of employee selection and placement, induction destress orientation at time of employment, employee counseling, training of employment interviewers, training of supervisors, prophylactic and psychobibliotherapy via books, referrals to social service agencies, and research. A seminal article entitled, "Mental Hygiene in Industry—A Clinical Psychologist's Contribution," was published in the *Journal of Clinical Psychology* in October 1947. A follow-up article, "Some Aspects of an Industrial Mental Hygiene Program," was published in the *Journal of Applied Psychology* in December 1951, and demonstrated that counseling cut the rate of turnover and increased employee satisfaction with the company.

I was invited to address approximately 5,000 safety engineers in Chicago at the National Safety Council Annual Convention in 1945. The topic was "Human Factors in Accidents." I made the point that there were psychological factors associated with accidents, and culled data from the literature. The paper was well received, and was published in the *Thirty-Sixth National Safety Congress Transactions* later in the year. Articles were also published in *Industrial Medicine, Psychosomatic Medicine, The American Journal of Orthopsychiatry,* and the *Journal of Clinical Psychology.*

In 1946, I received a phone call from Dr. Spafford Ackerly, professor and chairman of the Department of Psychiatry and Mental Hygiene, University of Louisville School of Medicine, inviting me to meet with him in New York City. Apparently, my colleague, Dr. Arthur Benton, with whom I had published my first article in 1941, had been associate professor of Medical Psychology at Louisville School of Medicine, and when he decided to move on to the University of Iowa as professor in their College of Medicine, recommended me as his replacement. Dr. Ackerly was then president of the American Orthopsychiatric Association, and I was honored to have lunch with him. He invited me to visit Louisville to meet the staff and for them to meet me.

I went, and after the weekend there, Dr. Ackerly offered me a position I could not refuse. I would be appointed associate professor of Medical Psychology, Department of Psychiatry and Mental Hygiene, University of Louisville School of Medicine, and chief psychologist, Norton Infirmary Department of Psychiatry. I would teach medical students, and be the first chief psychologist at the Norton Infirmary. I could examine patients and attend staff conferences at any of the facilities of the department at the Child Guidance Center or the General Hospital of the City of Louisville, and I would be the consultant at the VA Hospital, Department of Psychiatry. Of course, I could do independent research or join any team I would care to join. My activities were diversified and different from day to day. I learned much, participated in every aspect of the department, and contributed to the growth of an innovative phase of clinical psychology, namely, medical psychology, which today is also known as behavioral medicine, health psychology, and neurosciences.

My research culminated in several articles comparing the Binet to the Wechsler Intelligence Scale for Children; children's drawings, and editing the two-volume set: *Contributions Toward Medical Psychology*. One special mission in which I participated was to administer a comprehensive neuropsychodiagnostic test battery to two patients who were to get prefrontal lobotomies. Each patient was given the test battery before and after lobotomy on the right side and likewise on the left side. The data and test materials on these patients were elucidated at length with illustrations that demonstrate psychodynamic and psychopathological changes, and were used for teaching purposes. Other paradigm cases for teaching were thoroughly worked up and utilized with psychology interns and psychiatry and neurology residents.

In 1952, Dr. Thomas A. C. Rennie, professor of Psychiatry (Social Psychiatry), at Cornell University Medical College, whom I had known when I had my office in the Payne Whitney Building in 1942, asked whether I would be interested in joining a new interdisciplinary team created to study the effects of urban life on neuropsychiatric dysfunction. The team consisted of several psychiatrists, sociologists, social workers, anthropologists, trained interviewers, and biomedical statisticians. I was to exercise my expertise in psychological test construction and clinical psychology in developing a comprehensive questionnaire that would be administered to a large sample of respondents in their homes. The randomly selected sample consisted of 1,660 people residing in the catchment area surrounding the New York Hospital, from East Fifty-Ninth Street to East Ninety-Sixth Street, and from Fifth Avenue to the East River. The Yorkville Study became a classic of neuropsychiatric epidemiological research methodology and was published in two volumes dedicated to the memory of Dr. Rennie, who died just after the completion of the study. Volume One, *Mental Health in the*

Metropolis: The Midtown Manhattan Study (1962) and Volume Two, *Life Stress and Mental Health: The Midtown Manhattan Study* (1963), are still both read extensively and have been accepted with critical acclaim.

Returning to New York City afforded me an opportunity to resume my personal relationship with Dr. Wechsler. I was also asked to join the Second Division (Cornell) at Bellevue Hospital, Department of Neurology, and to become professor of Behavioral Sciences in the Bellevue School of Nursing. Years earlier, I had begun a syllabus for student nurses, but now I was adding additional behavioral sciences data, along with communication skills, cultural anthropology, and sociological and epidemiological information, which I felt would be useful to the nursing professional. Ultimately, I published two volumes, essentially for nurses and graduate students of the behavioral sciences. These were entitled: *Readings In Behavioral Sciences* and *Psychodiagnostic Methods For The Behavioral Sciences*. These were published in 1977.

I continued to teach these courses from 1952 to 1967, when the Bellevue School of Nursing, after more than 110 years, became part of the City University complex associated with Hunter College. The Bellevue School of Nursing had been founded in 1873 and was one of America's oldest and most distinguished nursing institutions. The school gave up its hallowed cap and pin, which was so much a part of its tradition for a century, when it merged with the City University of New York. Recognized for its exemplary training and nursing care by generations of physicians throughout our country and throughout the world, the Bellevue tradition still flourishes.

Another major reason for returning to the New York City area was to enter into my personal, didactic psychoanalysis. Dr. Bela Mittelmann, a training analyst, but also a colleague and personal friend, suggested that, rather than engaging in a traditional Freudian analysis with him, I enter into therapy with an Horneyian therapist. I interviewed several physicians and decided upon one who could see me three times a week at 7:30 A.M., and who was located on Upper Fifth Avenue. I was in therapy for three years and learned much about myself that would help me in my interpersonal relationships with close loved ones, patients, and students.

At the close of my personal therapy, my analyst suggested that I open my own office, dedicated to the neuropsychodiagnostic evaluation of patients, and do dynamic intensive psychoanalytically oriented psychotherapy with adolescents and adults. My supervision was arranged with Dr. Mittelmann on a weekly basis that lasted for approximately six years.

During this period, I would discuss, in-depth, patient material that required exploration into psychodynamic processes and how these impinged on progress in mental health. Patients were referred to me by lawyers, pediatricians, psychiatrists, psychoanalysts, neurologists, general practitioners, nurses, students, educators, counselors, other patients, and the B'nai B'rith College and Career Guidance Service, where I was appointed chief psychologist in 1961, part-time, and remained until July 1991.

My practice flourished. I attended many workshops and conventions, such as that of the American Psychological Association, Eastern Psychological Association, American Psychiatric Association, American Psychosomatic Society, American Neurological Association, and American Orthopsychiatric Association. I became a member of several of these, and authored about fifty articles in the journals they published. There were additional articles for popular consumption, such as a series of ten for *Parade Magazine* that went into eighteen million homes. These were on longitudinally psychologically developmental phases from infancy to geriatrics.

The nature of the scholarly articles covered a wide variety of topics that ranged from neuropsychodiagnostic test methods for pediatric physicians and medical students, to higher cortical levels of mentation, use of LSD and mescaline related to creativity, screening and selection techniques, underachievement, and the science teacher assays the underachiever. "The Way Our Children Play Can Save Their Mental Health" appeared in *Family Weekly*, and was seen by millions. Articles on underachievement, L-Dopa and its effects in Parkinsonism, and mental hygiene in industry were explored.

In August 1967, I delivered a paper at a Washington convention of B'nai B'rith vocational service counselors from throughout the country. The reporter who interviewed me from the *Washington Post* concluded: "Doctor Says Bad Students Spite Parents. Many students who don't do so well in school as they might are lagging behind just to spite their parents...some 'who are unwilling or unable to oppose their parents directly through argument or disobedience find academic failure an excellent means of expressing their suppressed rebellion.' '...A student often prefers being punished for not competing in school than trying to compete and failing...he'd rather be called lazy than stupid.'"

My article went on to summarize underachievers as students who sometimes come from families in which parents do not accept the child as an individual, penalize independent thinking, or regard a bright child as a competitor to be "cut down to size." Authoritarian parents sometimes "inhibit a child's independence, assertiveness, and spontaneity," and the child may retreat into underachievement as a result. The best way of helping them is to give them extensive testing, so they and parents will know their potential—assets as well as liabilities—and then not try to push them beyond these levels.

Apparently, the reporter put this article on the INS news wire, and the story was picked up by *The Voice,* a newspaper published by American Reform Judaism and the Christophers—a Catholic mass media organization which uses the printed word, television, and radio to spread two basic ideas: "There's nobody like you," and "You can make a difference." The Christopher message is based on the Judeo-Christian concept of service to God and all humanity. Its motto is: "Better to light one candle than to curse the darkness."

Each month, *Christopher News Notes* is sent to millions, and number 229 was entitled, "You're Really Something." It describes an American Indian legend in which a brave finds an eagle's egg and puts it into the nest of a prairie chicken. The eaglet hatched with the brood of chicks and grew up with them. All his life, the changeling eagle—thinking he was a prairie chicken—did what the prairie chickens did. He scratched in the dirt for seeds and insects to eat, he clucked and cackled, he flew no more than a few feet off the ground. After all, that's how prairie chickens were supposed to fly. Years passed. One day, he saw a magnificent bird flying gracefully. "What a beautiful bird!" said the changeling eagle to his neighbor. "What is it?"

"That's an eagle—the chief of the birds," the neighbor clucked. "But don't give it another thought. You could never be like him."

So the changeling eagle never gave it another thought. And it died thinking it was a prairie chicken.

The pamphlet goes on to quote Thoreau, Abraham Maslow, Carl Rogers, Isaiah, Franklin D. Roosevelt, and St. Paul, and concludes, "Underachievers are not born, they are made."

That's the view of Dr. Arthur Weider, a New York clinical psychologist. He has spent years evaluating the potential of thousands of youngsters aged fourteen to twenty-one. And he observed a lot of human potential not being utilized. "We have to impart to underachievers the message that there is hope to reverse the tide," he says. "Otherwise, as people mature, they modify their expectations—like shifting gears to a lower level of achievement."

Dr. Weider points out that, if people can find a goal in which they have a sincere interest and to which they can give themselves wholeheartedly, they may be amazed at what they can achieve. "Often, this goal has to be found by a trial-and-error system," he explains. "But when true commitment is found, it offers life's greatest satisfaction. How we view ourselves plays a vital role in how we choose to spend our lives. So, don't sell yourself short. You're really something."

In 1968, I was appointed senior supervising psychologist, Department of Psychiatry, and research psychologist, Department of Neurology, The Roosevelt Hospital, New York City, although my academic appointment actually read: assistant clinical professor of Medical Psychology, Department of Psychiatry, College of Physicians and Surgeons, Columbia University. I supervised psychological externs, coordinated group therapy in the patient's therapeutic community, and did research on Parkinsonism. L-Dopa therapy had just come into vogue during this period, and a group of us in the Neurology Department studied the effects of this drug on highest integrative mental functions in Parkinsonism. We found L-Dopa to produce significant improvement in both verbal and performance IQ scores, despite the fact that this disease decreases intellectual and motor performance.

Late in 1970, I was invited to examine a notorious patient who had received world-wide publicity and who was preparing a military defense as the chief culprit in the My Lai massacre. His name, of course, was Lieutenant William Calley. I am at liberty to quote from an article published by the syndicated correspondent, Jack Anderson, on "The Calley File," which appeared in the *New York Post* on May 23, 1972. I knew nothing about the contents of this news item until it was called to my attention months after I submitted my report to Lieutenant Calley's defense attorney, George Latimer.

Jack Anderson's article was datelined Washington and appeared in more than 200 newspapers. After it appeared, I was phoned by Mr. Anderson's legman, Jim Wooten, who asked me a few questions concerning some of the terminology I had used in the original report. No breach of doctor-patient confidence occurred, as the findings had already been published in newspapers throughout the country. What follows is the verbatim Jack Anderson article:

"Lt. William Calley was suffering from mental disorders, in the opinion of two eminent psychologists, at the time he led his troops on a shooting spree through the tragic village of My Lai. A military court singled him out as the chief culprit in the My Lai massacre. He was convicted specifically of murdering twenty-two civilians.

"Yet the two psychologists, working independently, came up with remarkably similar findings that Calley was mentally and emotionally unstable—and possibly even deranged—during the My Lai slaughter.

"Confronted with these findings, dignified old George Latimer, the former military appeals judge who was both father figure and chief counsel for Calley, considered an insanity defense. In its harshest terms, the question was: would Calley want to risk being branded as a murderer or madman? Both the lieutenant and Latimer decided irrevocably against claiming insanity. {Parenthetically, I would like to add here that neither Dr. Stammeyer nor I knew of the other's participation in these studies of Lt. Calley.}

"The psychological tests, conducted by Dr. Eugene Stammeyer of Washington, D.C., and Dr. Arthur Weider of New York City, were locked away and never presented as evidence to the military jury. We have now obtained copies of these suppressed documents, which shed new insights into Calley's condition on March 16,

THE CATALYST

1968—the day dozens of innocent men, women, and children were gunned down by American troops at My Lai.

"Both psychologists spent many hours secretly testing Calley. Dr. Weider, senior supervising psychologist at Roosevelt Hospital and a Life Fellow of the American Orthopsychiatric Association, wrote the sharpest opinion. He gave Calley a battery of tests, including an experimental one under marijuana, in September 1970.

"These 'reflect the psychopathology of a very serious personality and mental disorder which has the tendency to become full-blown and uncontrollable under such (circumstances) as may have existed at the My Lai atrocities,' wrote Weider. 'The possibility of a psychotic or prepsychotic condition must be considered...This patient's test results are suggestive of a serious psychotic condition.'

"Some of Calley's responses, such as a denial of indulgence in any 'unusual sex practices' and his feeling 'someone has been trying to influence my mind,' may require 'further investigation by the clinician,' added Weider.

"Dr. Stammeyer, a criminal psychologist expert at St. Elizabeth's hospital and lecturer at Catholic University, agreed that Calley had a 'potential for fragmentation of mental processes and anxiety attacks of near panic proportions when under limited stress...The picture of an overinhibited personality structure fraught with internal conflict between impulses and repressive forces is sharply etched...Paranoid trends could easily be aroused by stress.'

"Although Stammeyer stressed it would be difficult to describe Calley's exact condition on the day of the massacre, the distinguished criminal psychologist said: 'It is improbable that Lt. Calley was able to maintain...objective, rational control, being surrounded with horror, cruelty and violent death.' Calley's 'repressive defense' may well have been 'overwhelmed, releasing buried effects precipitating an emotional storm of rage, resentment, scorn, and hostile aggression.'

"Stammeyer traced Calley's instability back to his earliest childhood: 'He recalls being enuretic regularly until the age of five and continuing to periodically "wet his pants" through the second grade, suggesting a rooting of emotional conflicts in early childhood.

"His relationship with his father was 'distant.' Although he was closer to his mother, he found her 'an unusually ambitious, driving woman, relative lacking in emotional warmth...'Lt. Calley failed the seventh grade,' wrote Stammeyer. In view of the boy's native intelligence, this 'suggests a rather profound sense of alienation and estrangement,' the doctor said.

"Government psychiatrists, meanwhile, had found Calley 'normal.' This raises questions whether the government gives adequate psychological tests and why the Army placed a man of Calley's caliber in command of combat troops.

"Footnote: Latimer, reached in Salt Lake City, told us: 'Counsel and defendant were in agreement on not raising legal insanity as an issue. The issue was whether the horrors of combat were such as to impair, in a transitory way, a person's capacity to premeditate or have a specific intent to kill.'"

Thus ends Jack Anderson's article.

On June 12, 1973, I was asked to participate at a hearing at City Hall called by Mayor John Lindsay. I chose to talk on the topic, "Air Pollution and New York City." An abstract of my remarks follow:

"Man has been contaminating the atmosphere since he has inhabited this planet. However, only until recently has he had the good sense to consider air pollution a serious threat to his society. The effects of air pollution on health is well-known and obvious and its effects on man's psyche will also be established, I am sure.

"Civilization progresses by keeping babies alive, healing the sick, preventing sewage from getting into the water supply—one starts with doing things that are necessarily and intrinsically good. And how does one end? One ends by increasing the sum of human misery and jeopardizing civilization via the air he pollutes. Just as the chariot had to be banned in Ancient Rome—which has been given as one reason for the decline and fall of the Roman Empire—so, too, did our mayor have to ban the motor vehicle from lower Broadway—but, let's hope—with different results. Nonetheless, the exhaust fumes from the automobiles are the major cause of air pollution.

"If a man can not make a success on earth, he also may be unable to make himself a success anywhere else in the universe. It is a truism that evolution of the environment shapes the evolution of humanity.

"We shape our tools' thereafter our tools shape us.

"New York, my native city—and the greatest one of all the world—East Side, West Side...yet when Mayor Lindsay overheard lunarnauts Borman, Lovell, and Anders say, "It's a forbidding place...gray and colorless...it shows scars of a terrific bombardment...certainly not a very inviting place to live or work...," he said that for a chilling moment, he thought they were talking about New York.

"Let us enjoy man's survival tomorrow by planning for his breathing today! In the past twenty years, little serious attention has been given to the issue of pollution except some emissions testing, and none to global warming in America's major cities. Trucks and passenger cars may yet be banned in major center cities if no attention is given to pollution and these other warnings by current environmentalists."

During the end of 1973, the Cornell Index began to enjoy a resurgence of popularity, with requests for this quick screening test coming from all over our country and abroad. I was especially pleased when the New York Police Department included this test for all candidates to the force. I discovered this by accident when I was selected as a senior psychological consultant in the department and was sent a complete protocol on a questionable candidate and saw that the Cornell Index was part of the file. Since then, the NYPD has used this test with thousands of candidates, as well as the New York Transit Police Department.

To my great pleasure, the Cornell Index has come to enjoy an international reputation, and is used in places as diverse as Dublin, Ireland; Linkoping, Sweden; Bologna, Italy; Ministry of Defence, Tanglin, Singapore; and Australian Council for Educational Research, Victoria, Australia. In past years, requests have come from England, France, Egypt, Poland, Romania, and Russia. In America, such illustrious institutions as The National Institute of Mental Health, New York Psychiatric Institute, St. Vincent's Hospital in New York City and Westchester County, the Correctional Institute in Lima, Ohio, University of Tennessee, and General Motors of Michigan have inquired about it.

For more than forty-five years, I tried to maintain a very traditional, staid, professional practice as a neuropsychodiagnostician, psychotherapist, researcher, author, and professor. To a large degree, I believe I succeeded. My calendar was full with a practice daily from 8:00 A.M. till 9:00 or 10:00 P.M. frequently; and often Saturday and Sunday, until noon.

Throughout my career, I endeavored to have my offices close to my home and, more often than not, they were either in the same brownstone or in the same large apartment with a separate entrance. Thus, I was at home for my children, and frequently, even available to them. I did not commute, so I could close one door, open another, and be home. I saw my children in the mornings, after school, and in the evenings. They tell me now that they looked forward to cancellations as did I, even though I could never bring myself to charge patients in therapy for cancellations, as many of my colleagues did.

In many other ways, I was unorthodox in my practice. My motto always was: "I care." My patients knew that; they also knew that I am one of the few therapists who is available always, even in August. In addition, I never screen my calls and I answer the phone even during a session, because, "You never know when, in an emergency, you may need to talk to me."

THE CATALYST

I was considered to be so unorthodox by patients and colleagues alike that I had two shingles made up to read, "COME IN AND HAVE YOUR FAITH LIFTED," and the other, "SATISFACTION GUARANTEED OR YOUR MANIA RETURNED." I enjoyed my patients and they must have enjoyed me, for many stayed in therapy through changes, fruition, and toward mental health.

Generosity and altruism were characteristics known to me from early childhood. I recall that my father had a reputation of helping friends, relatives, and *landsleit*. He not only gave them non-interest-bearing loans, but gave them money for food and rent, and jobs, too. There were many Friday paydays when he came home with less funds than most of his employees and newly arrived emigres. This frequently resulted in an argument between my parents, which my father usually won with a hug or a remark of endearment. Indeed, on many Friday nights, our entire family, with extended members including grandmother, aunts, uncles, cousins, and these very same *landsleit*, would congregate at our flat to imbibe homemade wine, homemade cake, chickpeas, nuts and other goodies until the wee hours of the morning. While everyone had a good, loud time, none ever really got smashed nor drunk. Nonetheless, it was agreed that my parents knew how to entertain and make even strangers feel at home...it was known as *gemutlichkeit*.

And, so it was that I enjoyed entertaining and having guests eat and drink and be merry. I, too, loaned students, friends, and patients sums of money, which they frequently returned as promised, although there are still a few such loans outstanding. I guess I was considered an easy touch when a patient needed funds for a telephone bill or a doctor's bill, or when a friend wanted to return to Japan to visit his aged mother so that she could see her new grandchildren. I enjoyed the opportunity to do good beyond the call of my profession; indeed, loaning money to patients might have been considered ill-advised and even unethical, but not in the '60s.

In the spring of 1975, I received a phone call from a young woman who wanted to consult me regarding her boyfriend. She arrived on time for the appointment and related the fact that she was a nurse at an East Side hospital and was in love with a man "who was floundering about, undecided what to do about his career." He phoned me for an appointment and appeared reluctantly to talk about himself. I guess I was supposed to know who he was, but I confessed to him I did not. He was Art Heyman, a former New York Knick, first draft for his year and a three-time All-American basketball player from Duke who had some records that still stood; a legend in the Southeast Conference. He had been divorced and had closed a restaurant, and was undecided as to what to do with his life; not that he had not had offers. He could return to Durham, where he was well-known, and open a restaurant, or go to Duke Law School, where he claimed he had been accepted, or go to New Orleans and accept some job representing a restaurant chain, or stay in New York City and get some backing to open another restaurant.

Later that week, a young woman who came for her weekly appointment related what she called an interesting set of events. Immediately after having had intercourse, her partner roused and jumped out of the bed and exclaimed, apropos of nothing, that he would love to own a restaurant. Finding this rather unusual, she thought she should remember this and tell me about it the very next time she saw me. I heard what she had said, and filed this bit of information in her record.

Some days later, Art Heyman appeared again, depressed and aimless and at wit's end. He felt that time was running out, and he must make a decision; he was an impatient man, I noted. Before he left, he stated that he would like to have another fling at running a restaurant in New York City and not leave the town where he was known so well. While I was listening to him, the visualization of that other young man jumping out of bed after intercourse and exclaiming that he wanted to own a restaurant came to my mind. I smiled and it must have been noticeable to Art, because he asked me what was so funny. Of course, I did not let on, but I did say that I might know someone who might be interested in backing him in a restaurant. I asked him if I had his permission to set up an appointment for him to meet this man Sunday afternoon, in the living room of my apartment at the Eldorado on Central Park West, overlooking the reservoir on the twenty-third floor.

In this enchanting environment, on a beautiful Sunday afternoon in the early spring, practically in the clouds with seagulls flying about, Art came first, followed by Joel Korby, attired in white tennis shorts with his hand-knitted sweater drawn around his broad shoulders. I had not met the latter and had no idea what he would be like. These two strangers shook hands and began to chat as though they had known one another since their adolescence. Obviously, Joel was impressed with Art, whose career he had followed while in high school and college; he had known of him as a Knick, also. As a matter of fact, Joel had played varsity basketball, also, but admittedly not in Art's league. They hit it off famously!

About the restaurant...oh, yes. Art and Joel exchanged addresses and phone numbers and agreed to meet during the upcoming week, and Art stated he would begin to check with brokers he knew who specialized in locating restaurants. It sounded as though he could deliver, and Joel could arrange the financing. They both insisted that there should be a place for me in this alliance. My wisdom, maturity, and perspicacity were qualities they wanted...my money came later!

I saw this as an opportunity to take my life into new directions and meet challenges I never before had to meet. Having been scholarly and professorial, this was an opportunity to be extroverted, epicurean, and hedonistic. Besides, hidden in every man's unconscious is the wish to own a restaurant! It must be ego.

Within the week, we had looked at five or six different restaurants and, for one reason or another, rejected all six. Art, the impatient one, would have agreed to all six. Joel had more sense and determination. I had some objections and opinions also.

Joel was a successful businessman, and he and his brother were running an import-carrying-case business in the South Bronx. He had experience and knew what was involved in operating a business; besides, he had majored in Business Administration, and I could see he was very obsessive and compulsive in his habits and note-taking. Joel was responsible, prompt, and reliable. Art was quite the opposite; he was unreliable, late, and irresponsible. Together, they were truly the "odd couple." I was their therapist, but *sans* fee!

Late one afternoon, I got a phone call from Art, who told me to meet him and Joel and a lady broker friend of his at a townhouse on East Forty-Eighth Street, off First Avenue. At six o'clock, we were shown into a luxurious, renovated four-story brownstone townhouse. In the basement was a large spacious disco outfitted with the latest state-of-the-art speakers and turntables with records and lighting equipment. On the first floor street level was a fine restaurant with unusually expensive-looking brocaded chairs and matching banquettes and draperies. On the walls, which were covered with fine fabrics, were museum-quality oil paintings that were lighted from above each picture. The doors and wood were the finest mahogany with brass fittings. The bar lounge appeared to be an old English pub clubroom, with a large, copper-covered bar with glasses to fix every variety of drink. The refrigerators below the bar were of the finest quality. The lights on the walls were English sconces with dimmers. The rugs were tailor-made for the entire room, in startlingly expensive taste. In the very rear of this floor was a professionally outfitted kitchen, with every convenience one could imagine for such a business-like restaurant kitchen. There were walk-in refrigerators, ice machines, cutting equipment of every sort, liquor, canned goods, bar needs, glasswares, table settings, and eating utensils. In short, no money was spared to outfit the building, the rooms, and the furnishings, all in exquisite taste.

On the second floor, there was a wood-panelled library stocked with books on a large variety of subjects. The couches and chairs were large, tufted, richly appointed, beautifully matched, and unashamedly comfortable, in keeping with the expensive impression of all of the interiors. Backgammon tables, made to order for this backgammon club, along with other gaming tables, were smartly placed in the room. Toward the rear of this floor was a large lounge area with mirrored walls on all sides and a miniature dance floor with speakers carrying music from the basement, so that disco or good, old-fashioned ballroom dancing was available.

On the third floor was a large Jacuzzi, big enough for twenty people. Next to this wondrous accoutrement was a large Swedish sauna that could accommodate at least six adults. Swedish showers were available for at least ten people.

On the top floor was a storage area and a large gymnasium with every conceivable exercise equipment that comprised a complete Universal weights and body building apparatus. Lockers for fifty people lined the remaining walls of this fourth floor, along with the personnel office.

On the roof of this nirvana was a fabulous roof garden, two regulation platform tennis courts built on wood decking, all enclosed with high see-through wire meshing to keep the tennis balls from leaving the courts, and a completely equipped flexible bar.

By the time we reached the roof, all three of us were convinced that we would not let this opportunity get away. We knew we wanted it...all of it! Genesis, a private club, had been founded by a famous Japanese playboy for the sole purpose of having a backgammon tournament available in New York City; all the rest of this townhouse was for the pleasure of the club members. In the early '70s, the economy took a turn for the worse and it was difficult to maintain such a club for more than a few years. The net lease was available for twenty-one years at a relatively low monthly rental. There were no restrictions on the uses of the building or the rooms, or on the zoning.

Within a week, the lawyers drew up the necessary contracts and Opus One was founded. All licenses were applied for, as Art knew his way around the State Liquor Authority, and we prepared to open a fine, elegant French Continental restaurant. Joel and I would double as hosts, and we hired female and male models to wait tables. We had a gala bash opening, with the Who's Who of New York City appearing at three different sittings. We three had our restaurant. It was a huge success, but it lasted only six months. After New Year's Eve, 1975, we all had the same brainstorm. We would close and, after much hoopla, reopen as a multilevel, three-tiered disco with three bars. We would charge only $5.00 for admission. I got the brilliant ad campaign that went like this: "Why Settle For A Studio When You Can Have A Townhouse?"

You see, we changed our concept from a restaurant to three discos: Townhouse 48! Townhouse 48 was a fabulous place for young people to come to meet, congregate, dance, and have a great time inexpensively. I saw it as group activity therapy, far cheaper than the going rates for psychotherapy. Everyone had a fine, healthy time under the best security surveillance, and illicit drugs were strictly verboten. Studio 54 was then our only competition.

THE CATALYST

The famous and not-so-famous came, and many came each and every Friday and Saturday. Our music was up-to-date and well-mixed, and word got around in the city, suburbs, and even out in the hinterlands that our discos "were out of this world, super." A young Hispanic man of eighteen from the South Bronx appeared with milk crates full of records who wanted a job mixing in Manhattan as a disc-jockey. We gave him his start, Jelly-Bean Benetiz, now world-famous as the original arranger for Madonna. He has gigs in Hollywood, does movies and records, and performs all over the world, and when he sees me he genuflects and "kisses my ring" under my eyes, that is. No, he really hugs me as though he means it. Most of our clientele believed I looked like Topper or Leo G. Carroll; I thought I resembled Don Ameche, but that was before their time, so the name Topper stuck to me and, even to this day, When I am recognized, I am called Topper. I knew then that they were habitués of the disco era; not students, nor patients, nor clients.

This period in my life was a renaissance of sorts, for me! Townhouse 48 flourished and thrived. It was a success, and many young types enjoyed themselves and danced the whole night in a healthy, supervised ambience.

Joel looked after the running of the club, as it really required a businessman and not a jock. I enjoyed the entire experience of seeing healthy exuberance spill over the several dance floors and young people in various forms of self-expression actually having a good time for so little cost.

Art was bored with the lack of action and, besides, he wanted a restaurant. As luck would have it, one became available at his old hunting ground and he arranged to be bought out by Joel so that he could make his wish come true. He insisted, however, that I join him in this new venture and also keep a piece of Townhouse 48 with Joel. So, early in 1976, I was co-owner of Arthur's Court, an "in" restaurant on the fashionable upper East Side, and co-owner of the disco on Forty-Eighth Street.

My clinical practice continued unabated, but many of my evenings were relegated to seeing people getting well-fed and others getting healthy exercise through contemporary dancing. I sacrificed no one...neither patients, clients, family, nor customers. Furthermore, I was meeting celebrities, neighbors, published authors, columnists, musicians, vocalists, actors and actresses, athletes, and community leaders.

A day or two before Thanksgiving, Art introduced me to George Vecsey, a prestigious *New York Times* columnist who had just finished a book, *The Coal Miner's Daughter*, a biography written with Loretta Lynn about the country singer's tumultuous life. Apparently, George came to interview me for a possible story. On Saturday, November 27, 1976, the following appeared in the venerable *New York Times*:

"Dr. Arthur Weider, a psychologist and owner of Arthur's Court restaurant, points out attraction of the menu to passers-by on First Avenue."

THE CATALYST

The heading of the article: "A Dose of Applied Psychology Draws Diners and Feeds an Ego."

"Many restaurant proprietors insist that they are amateur psychologists, but Arthur Weider, the man cajoling customers on First Avenue, is a professional.

"Seven days a week, Dr. Weider practices as a clinical psychologist from his Manhattan apartment, dealing with the woes of modern, urban people. Several evenings a week, he tells total strangers to 'eat, enjoy, be happy'—preferably at his restaurant.

"The restaurant is Arthur's Court, at First Avenue and Seventy-Sixth Street. As people scurry by on cool evenings, they may see three figures standing outside: Arthur Heyman, the former basketball player with Duke University and the New York Knickerbockers, is the tall one in charge of rebounding and defense; Arthur the Knight is the suit of armor supporting the menu board (he doesn't talk much); Dr. Arthur Weider is the trim-mustached 'fatherly type,' smiling near a table of menus. Even if the weather dips below freezing, Dr. Weider is smiling.

"'I need this restaurant,' Dr. Weider said. 'I listen almost all day, although I am not a passive Freudian, either. But at night, I've got a bunch of words that have to come out. I like to meet people. I like to arrange them, choreograph them, make them happy.'

"He also likes to charm the customers off the sidewalks. This is why Mr. Heyman, his partner, calls him 'The Hook.' A couple can be walking along First Avenue dreaming of Thai food, French food, Brazilian food, and whoops, suddenly they are seated in Arthur's Court, under a hand-painted, pseudo-medieval banner, inspecting the menu.

"'To tell you the truth, I mesmerize them,' Dr. Weider said. "I go from suggestion to reinforcement to levity to appetite to economy in a spectrum of five points. If they say they want atmosphere, I promise them atmosphere 'til it's coming out of their ears. And by the way, our food is excellent.'

"To be sure, Dr. Weider is not spellbinding people into munching on sawdust or nails. Back in the kitchen, he has dragooned the irrepressible Christian Johnson, who whips up zucchini-and-escarole soup in slow moments. The restaurant's eclectic menu includes 'overstuffed' sandwiches in the four-dollar-range and salads from $3.25 that boast of raw broccoli, red cabbage, turnip dressings, whole artichoke hearts, and other vegetable delights. There is also 'Lusty, Lusty Lamb' at $5.75.

"'Hey, let me tell you what the Doc did last week,' said John Garth, the bartender. "A guy walks by, alone, eating a slice of pizza.

The Doc looks at him and says, "You really don't want to eat pizza." In five minutes, the guy was sitting down ordering a four-course meal. That man is unreal.'

"On a slow Tuesday night recently, the doctor (a Ph.D., actually) showed how he operates. He spied Gloria Magat, an energy expert, waiting on the corner, looking indecisive, and he called out, 'Dear, here's the menu.' Mrs. Magat strolled over and inspected the menu while Dr. Weider instructed her to consult the 'penultimate page.' When Mrs. Magat smiled, Dr. Weider told her she would pass her S.A.T.s (an achievement test) if she knew that word. Mrs. Magat said she was supposed to meet her husband elsewhere. Dr. Weider called after her, 'Bring him back with you.' Along came Richard Magat, also alone, looking for his wife. Dr. Weider said, "You must be a doctor.' Mr. Magat replied that he was an editor, but he seemed pleased anyway. Mr. Magat said he was supposed to meet his wife and another couple in a nearby restaurant. Dr. Weider turned a little green in the gills, as if to suggest 'that place is just a glorified coffee shop.' He told the departing Mr. Magat to bring the whole gang back with him.

"Inside, Artie Heyman pulled a $10 bill and said, 'They won't come back.' Dr. Weider matched the bet. A few minutes later, the Magats returned with two friends, Elliot Solomon and Dianne Robinson.

"Benevolent Electricity

"'A little benevolent electricity goes a long way in New York City,' Mr. Solomon said. 'The idea of someone being friendly totally reverses a New Yorker. We're always dealing with muggers and hookers, we're not prepared for somebody nice. But Dr. Weider does not talk to just anybody.'

"'I only talk to intelligent people,' he explained. 'If they smile when I tell them I have a Ph.D., I think they'll like the food. I won't operate with morons.'

"Not that he wants every sharpy on First Avenue to hustle him, but Dr. Weider has been known to subsidize a first meal for an impoverished couple. Lauren Silver, an art student, and Jeffrey Nissim, a classical guitar student, having one dollar between them, wanted to share one glass of wine in the outdoor cafe last summer. Dr. Weider let them linger at a table during a busy time, and they each got a full glass of wine. Needless to say, they have since returned because they love the food, too.

"The Doctor's Prescription

"'I love to put people at the right tables.' Dr. Weider said. "If a couple is arguing when they enter, I'll put them right in the middle of the room so they can't argue. They just can't. Then I send over a glass of wine.'

"Dr. Weider said that most of his patients know of his restaurant and many drop over for a meal. But, he added, 'I do not talk business in a restaurant,' and he said he was not looking for new cases, paid or unpaid, at the restaurant."

George Vecsey's article was read the world over, and favorable responses came from all over the country, Bermuda, and England. Indeed, many colleagues living in the city and nearby suburbs and states came to see one of their peers daring "to do his thing." Many expressed their desire to own a restaurant, but their nurturing was limited to therapy and dealing with food for thought, only. Many years later, when I would attend learned scientific conventions, colleagues from all over the country would make references to the restaurant and the article they had read in *The New York Times* in 1976. During 1976 and 1977, I shuttled between academe, private practice, hospital rounds, restaurant, disco, and the television studio.

In 1977, I published another two volumes: *Readings in Behavioral Sciences* and *Psychodiagnostic Methods for the Behavioral Sciences*. Both of these enjoyed adoptions at undergraduate and graduate-level college courses as well as by libraries throughout the country. Special courses in medical, nursing, and psychiatric programs utilized these volumes in courses and for reference.

From the '70s until 1983, I had an academic appointment as assistant clinical professor of Medical Psychology, Department of Psychiatry, College of Physicians and Surgeons, Columbia University, although I was stationed at the Roosevelt Hospital where I attended rounds, saw patients, supervised psychology externs, and did therapy in groups as part of the therapeutic community.

My career took another serendipitous turn when a former radio and television personality inquired as to my availability to do a television call-in program. This was in 1976, and as far as I knew, none of my colleagues in media psychology had undertaken this new medium, not even on radio; except that Dr. Ruth Westheimer was talking about sex. After being on television for almost a year and having built up quite a following of fans, complete with fan mail, we were approached by *The Village Voice*, which wanted to do a piece about our program, to be written by Clark Whelton. The following article appeared on October 3, 1977, entitled: "They Came from New Jersey"

"President Jimmy Carter White House Washington, D.C. 20500

Dear President Carter: My name is Larry McCann and I'm the producer of a new television show in New York called 'UFO Update.' My audience would like to know more about your campaign promise to divulge everything you know about UFOs and your own personal sightings and we are anxiously awaiting your reply.'"

THE CATALYST

In the center of the article was a five-by-seven picture with an inset of me. Under the picture the caption read: "Larry McCann, host of 'UFO Update,' and Dr. Arthur Weider, 'the People's Psychologist,' appear regularly on the 'All-Nite Show.'"

What follows is the article in its entirety.

"Larry McCann opened the door to the silver limousine. I stepped inside and settled down on the plush upholstery. Al, the chauffeur, turned around and told us that there would be a brief delay in getting underway. The People's Psychologist had gone up the block to buy some biscuits and jam for a late-night snack, but would be right back. Larry McCann checked his watch. We had plenty of time to get out to New Jersey. It wasn't even midnight yet, and 'UFO Update' didn't go on the air until two o'clock in the morning. But McCann wasn't taking any chances. He leaned forward and tapped on the partition glass.

"'Al,' he said. 'Drive up the block. We'll pick up the Doc on the way.'

"Al eased the silver limousine out into traffic and immediately spotted the People's Psychologist coming down MacDougal Street with a paper bag in his hand. The door opened. The People's Psychologist climbed inside and flipped up one of the jump seats. Larry McCann introduced me to Dr. Arthur Weider, a regular guest on McCann's 'All-Nite Show,' a two-hour program in which 'UFO Update is a thirty-minute segment. As 'the People's Psychologist,' Dr. Weider takes phone calls from troubled viewers between 3 and 4 A.M. 'Holland Tunnel, Al,' Larry McCann said, and a few minutes later we were cruising under the Hudson. The People's Psychologist had opened his bag of biscuits and was busy prying the lids off plastic tubs of marmalade. Al steered the limousine onto the Pulaski Skyway. 'We're not going straight to the studio,' McCann said. 'First I'm stopping off at my folks' place near Summit to pick up another car.'

"'Have you heard from President Carter yet?' I asked.

"McCann shook his head. 'The president didn't answer my first telegram,' he said. 'So I sent him another one.'

"*Dear President Carter: I have a vast audience on my television program, 'UFO Update,' shown in New York over WTVG/TV, Channel 68, and they have the right to know if our military forces have ever engaged in combat with a UFO. General Benjamin Chiclaw has revealed that the Air Force has lost many men and aircraft pursuing UFOs. I would appreciate a speedy reply to this telegram since the volume of mail from my viewers regarding this matter has been overwhelming and they would like to have an answer.*

"'I finally received a form letter from the air force,' McCann said. 'It was full of the usual denials. "There are no UFOs; we have no record of planes being lost." But I'm going to keep after the president. He's the key to this thing.'

"McCann told me that he has been doing 'UFO Update' since he went on the air with the 'All-Nite Show' last April. Before that, Mc-Cann was a disc jockey with WPIX. He has also been a singer and actor and still does lots of voice-overs. A couple of years ago, he wrote a UFO novel called *The Master Plan*, which is now being vocally dramatized on 'UFO Update.' (The viewers are told that each 'Master Plan' installment is found in a waterfront phone booth.)

"McCann told me that things were going well for the 'All-Nite Show'. He had picked up a few new sponsors, including the East Wind Limousine Service, which had provided the car in which we were riding.

"'Hey, Doc.' Larry McCann said. 'Does Reggie Jackson still come to Arthur's Court?'

"'Oh, sure,' the People's Psychologist replied. 'Reggie was there tonight. He's been under a lot of pressure. It helps him to relax.'

"Larry McCann explained that, besides being a clinical psychologist, Dr. Weider runs two night spots in Manhattan: Arthur's Court, a restaurant on First Avenue and the Townhouse, a discotheque on East Forty-Eighth Street. 'You're not seeing Reggie as a patient, are you Doc?' Larry McCann asked. "'Oh, no,' the People's Psychologist replied. 'But I talk to him when he comes in. You know, build up his confidence.'

"At Newark Airport, McCann directed the limousine around an enormous cloverleaf and onto an expressway which, as far as I knew, didn't exist. I checked my bearings. There were now six lanes of cement where Maplewood used to be. Rain splashed against the wind-shield. I began to get a little nervous.

"'Have you ever seen a UFO?' I asked Larry McCann.

"'No, but I'd sure like to see one,' he replied. 'How about you?'

"I told him that I had never seen a UFO, although I once encountered a mysterious light in the sky near Danbury, Connecticut. It turned out to be a star. And several years before that I had dropped in on a Flying Saucer Convention. I remember a man selling vials of Martian sand, a woman in a suit made of blue feathers, a barber from Brooklyn who received intergalactic bulletins on his bridgework, and a grandmother who was peddling a piece of autobiographical reportage entitled *My Venusian Lover*. It was your typical cross-section of hard-core kooks, but here were thousands of them. Thousands!

"The miles rolled by. I began to eye a console of buttons and switches on my side of the limousine. It looked like Captain Kirk's dashboard. I opened a small sliding panel and a light popped on. I slammed it shut.

"'What else have you been up to lately, Doc?' Larry McCann asked. The People's Psychologist turned around.

"'The Queens D.A. has asked me to examine David Berkowitz.'

"'Son of Sam?' McCann said. 'Is that right? Wow! Did you see in the paper that dozens of women have been writing love letters to that guy?'

"'They're wasting their time,' the People's Psychologist said. 'There's nothing in his pistol. He can only shoot blanks.'

"'Now, wait a minute, Doc. You haven't examined him yet.'

"'No, but I've been following the case closely,' the People's Psychologist replied.

"Al took the limousine down an exit ramp and we began to follow local roads. It was well after midnight, and the rain was coming down harder. The People's Psychologist was talking about a friend who got rich by inventing Aspergum and Feenamint. I was trying to figure out where we were. At last the limousine stopped on a dark street. Larry McCann went to get the second car. Al went with him.

"I returned my attention to the panel of switches. I fooled around with the climate control, the private radio dials, the ashtray and lighter, and the row of buttons. Windows went up and down. There was a loud clicking sound. Al, the chauffeur, came back, tried the door, and said, 'Hey, you locked me out.'

"'Good grief. One of the switches must have been the automatic door lock.'

"I pushed another button. Another window went down.

"'Never mind,' Al said, 'I got the keys.'

"He turned the limousine around. We followed Larry McCann deeper into New Jersey.

"'Have you ever been to the Townhouse?' the People's Psychologist asked. I told him that I didn't disco very often. 'It's the poor man's psychotherapy,' he said. 'You should try it.' He told me that his discotheque had originally been called Genesis, but had also been called Opus, The Experiment, and finally, The Townhouse.

"'Why so many changes?' I asked.

"'People get bored. They like new places, so we change the name. WE also change clientele quite frequently. Originally we were straight. Then we went gay. Next we went black. Now we're back to straight again, but *elegant* straight this time.'

"'How do you control your clientele?'

THE CATALYST

"'It all depends on word of mouth and where you advertise. When we went gay, we hired a gay manager who brought his friends. When we went black, we advertised on WBLS.'

"As the People's Psychologist talked about discotheques, I glanced out the window. I still couldn't figure out where the hell we were. The houses had electric lights and the roads were paved, which I took as a good sign. When I looked back at the People's Psychologist he was talking about the time he examined Lieutenant William Calley and, before I could ask my next question, the limousine turned off the road and stopped. I opened the door. We were in front of what looked like a small house with a parking lot for a front yard. Looming almost directly above us was a 200-foot broadcast tower. Next door was a long, low building with a sign that said, 'SUPER DISCO.' Down the road were the lights of a bowling alley. Directly across the street was a dark patch of forest primeval, complete with crickets.

"Larry McCann scooped an armful of videotaped advertisements out of the trunk and took them inside. The house was both studio and transmitter for WTVG/TV, Channel 68. The studio looked like an average attic. All kinds of junk was piled in the corners. Chairs and props were scattered around the room, which was about the size of a sun porch.

"The background set for the *Stock Market Today* program was folded against one wall. I looked up. The ceiling and walls had been upholstered with shaggy carpet. A carpet-covered desk was pushed into one corner next to a couple of plastic holly plants. Pointing at the desk were two television cameras, one of which had a TV set strapped to the top to show what it was aimed at.

"Larry McCann opened a door and went into the control room. Three men were watching *All the President's Men* on the transmitter monitor. WTVG specializes in broadcasting first-run movies in a scrambled signal to subscribers who rent special decoders that iron out the image. At 2 A.M., the scrambled movie will be over and 'UFO Update' will be on the air, unscrambled. I checked the control-room clock. An hour to go.

"While Larry McCann got his ad tapes lined up, I snooped around the building. The People's Psychologist was seated at a desk upstairs, talking on the phone. He hung up as I approached.

"'I just called New York,' he said. 'We had 400 people in the Townhouse tonight. That's a nice crowd.'

"Larry McCann came upstairs with the 'UFO Update' fan mail in his hand. A woman from East Rutherford had a complaint.

"'*Dear Larry: I find it very sad that you cannot promote the idea of UFOs. There are many of us who become bored with the ignorant phone calls you receive and the simplicity of our still-ignorant people. Larry, you yourself know exactly what you're talking about and yet you have to lower your level to reach those unbelievers. I am referring to what you often say, 'A NEW LEVEL OF CONSCIOUSNESS.'*

"McCann opened another letter. I went downstairs. Standing in the studio was a man with a boa constrictor wrapped around his neck. The snake's name was Julius Squeezer, the man told me, as the boa's tongue darted in and out in the approved serpent style. The snake was definitely eyeballing my left arm. I backed off. Larry McCann came into the room and introduced me to Neil Padron from Petland in New York. Petland is one of his sponsors and also provides the animals for a portion of the 'All-Nite Show' called: 'Pet Care.' Tonight's pets are Julius Squeezer and a surly-looking bird called a sulfur-crested cockatoo. 'Pet Care' has replaced a popular feature called: 'The Night Owl Astrologer,' which is temporarily off the air. I checked my watch. Thirty minutes to 'UFO Update.'

"McCann began to move furniture around the room, straightening up the set. He lined up the carpet-covered desk and the two plastic holly plants and dragged the other junk out of camera range. A man came out of the control room to admire Julius Squeezer. He touched a lump on the snake's waist.

"'What's this?' he asked.

"'Two mice,' Neil Padron replied.

"The man's hand shot back. Fifteen minutes until 'UFO Update.'

"The People's Psychologist sat down on a chair by the door. Larry McCann took his sport jacket out of a plastic bag and smoothed the lapels. On the transmitter monitor Nixon was resigning. Larry McCann sat down behind the desk. He took a deep breath, then got up to check the cameras. During the show, McCann told me, he can't move around because there is only one engineer in the studio and the cameras are unmanned. They just point.

"McCann went into the control room to review the show's material again. First would come the introduction, then the announcement that President Carter has still not replied to the requests for UFO information, then a long monologue about Sir Eric Gairy, Prime Minister of the Island of Grenada, who has asked the United Nations to investigate UFOs. Sir Eric has been invited to appear on the October 7 show. Then cut to the special taped feature by Bryce Bond, a UFO researcher. Bond's subject tonight is UFO artist Mark Brinckerhoff, who paints scenes of life in other galaxies, thanks to the telepathic inspiration he receives from outer space. Then cut to the dramatization of 'The Master Plan.' Then cue for sign off.

"McCann went back to the shaggy desk. At the rear of the room the sulfur-crested cockatoo was keeping his eye on Julius Squeezer, which was still wrapped around Neil Padron's neck. The People's Psychologist was standing by the door. Outside in the rain, Al the chauffeur was sitting in the silver limousine.

"'Now!' somebody shouted through the control-room door.

"'Good evening,' Larry McCann said, 'and welcome to "UFO Update." "UFO Update" can be seen Friday evening at 2 A.M. on channel 68, channel "M" if you have cable.'"

October 1977 was a momentous month for me, New Yorkers, and the New York Yankees in particular. I should say that Arthur's Court was a favorite watering hole for many professional athletes of New York teams, especially basketball and baseball stars. One frequent customer was Reggie Jackson, newly acquired by the New York Yankees. He enjoyed our outdoor cafe where he could have a salad and coffee or a beer and keep an eye on his Rolls parked at a meter or usually just double-parked.

During the late summer of 1977, Heyman and I planned to introduce jazz at our restaurant, and as an inaugural event, we invited many of the Yankees to be our guests at a well-publicized Saturday evening, October 8. Prophetically, or just plain luck, it turned out that the Yankees were almost assured of winning the American League Pennant that afternoon, so that our event planned many months before actually turned out to be a victory bash. Our M.C. was Reggie, himself, who brought along Fran Healy and Lou Piniella. We were jammed, and the local East Sider sports people were thrilled, especially since the Yankees did win their pennant the next day and were in the World Series, which began on October 11, 1977.

Usually, when his team was in town, Reggie would come in for his salad and beer; the World Series was no different. On an afternoon of a day which, I am sure, will live forever in his memory, as well as in the memory of many Yankee fans, he came by and I went out to his car. He asked if he could have his salad and a six-pack of Heineken to go. He remained in his car, and I left to give the order. When I returned he asked, "What do I owe you, Doc?"

"Just one home run, Reggie." He smiled and left.

The rest is history, as they say! The *New York Times* sent a young reporter, Robert McG. Thomas, Jr., who wrote an article that appeared on Thursday, October 20, 1977. It follows:

"Waiting for Reggie"

"The Chipmunk was waiting for Reggie Jackson. Jersey Joe was waiting for Reggie Jackson. John the Hog and Goosedown Gary were waiting for Reggie Jackson; the Playboy Club bunnies, Bunny Bander and Bunny Spill, were waiting for Reggie Jackson and, once he'd got his cab precisely double-parked so that it blocked a Lincoln

THE CATALYST

Continental and a ramshackle van, Michael J. Nolan was waiting for Reggie Jackson, too.

"Nolan got out of his cab wearing a Yankee batting helmet and lugging a substitute souvenir of the Yankee victory. Having mislaid his Stadium ticket stub he happily seized on the expedient nearest to hand, or there abouts, and simply not let go of his seat when he got up to leave after the last pop bunt.

"Now, tucking his blue plastic plunder under his arm, he strolled into Arthur's Court, a bar-restaurant and jazz emporium at First Avenue and Seventy-Sixth Street, where, at 1:30 in the morning, a few score revelers awaited its most celebrated knight. They were all waiting for Reggie Jackson, but nobody was waiting as much as the girl with red hair.

"'His girlfirend is waiting for him, so we know he's going to come,' confided Arthur Heyman, the one-time Knick and now a restaurateur, who is the taller of Arthur's Court's two Arthurs. The other, or Art Two, is Dr. Arthur Weider, a psychologist. Heyman and Weider were more than doubly certain that Reggie would show up. After all, Arthur's Court had been the superstar's favorite hangout ever since that sunny day last May when he was driving one of his Rolls-Royces up First Avenue and spotted the Court's sidewalk cafe and knew instantly that it would be a perfect place to sit and see and be seen.

"'Reggie likes pretty girls and we get a lot of them in here,' said Weider. Wasn't it right here a full four months ago—and Heyman swears it is so—that Jackson announced that he would finish the season with thirty homeruns and 100 runs batted in and then be named the most valuable player of the World Series?

"Hadn't he been here the night before, ordering a chef's salad the way he always does? And when he asked, 'Doc, how much do I owe you?' didn't Weider reply, as always, 'Just one home run, Reggie?' 'He's got to come,' someone said, 'Doc owes him two chef's salads.' And hadn't the chef, himself, been listening on the kitchen radio just two hours ago when Reggie announced that he was going to celebrate right here at Arthur's Court? And so they waited.

"John the Hog became the first victim of the evening, slumping to the bar about 3:30, but this simply gave heart to the others. They were so busy telling each other that Jackson was on his way that nobody noticed that the girl with red hair had gotten up from her table and slipped away.

"It was almost four o'clock. A young customer pulled out a picture made only five hours earlier showing Jackson in full batting stride, stroking the homerun that, someone noted, would make him a Yankee forever.

"Babe Ruth hit three homeruns in World Series games twice in 1926 and again in 1928 (hitting sixty during the regular season in between) and if Jackson is the competitor those in Arthur's Court know him to be, he'll need to stay on a World Series team."

And so ends the article.

Addendum: A few days later, Reggie surfaced at Arthur's Court and I asked him what he had on his mind before hitting the first homerun. "The first one was for God; the second for my mother, and the third for your salad!"

In subsequent visits to our restaurant in the off-season, we had ample time to reminisce with Reggie when, in the beginning, he was so depressed and down because he felt he had to demonstrate that he was worth the money Mr. Steinbrenner paid for him. Reggie always felt it would be difficult to live up to their expectations and, besides, how many homeruns does one have to hit and how many runs need to be batted in for such large sums of money?

All this changed during that World Series night, and it's in the record books! Sometime during July 1978, Reggie, Billy Martin, and George Steinbrenner were not getting along. Indeed, all of the Yankees were in dire straits. Towards the end of July, Billy was fired (for the first time) and, in a depressed state, went off to fish in Minnesota. Somehow he got from Reggie a sheet of paper with Arthur's Court, the address, and my name on it. This was odd, as he and Reggie were already not getting on at all.

In any case, one afternoon, a black stretch limousine parks in front of the restaurant and out steps the one and only Billy Martin, in the flesh. He asks for me, and obviously, I'm beside myself and, with outstretched hand, welcome him to Arthur's Court. He orders a drink, and we sit down in a rather secluded spot to chat. He looks good but feels miserable, and I begin to build up his ego by telling him that he's one of the greatest managers of all time and that I go back to McGraw, McCarthy, and Casey Stengel. Furthermore, I tell him he's not down and out and that he'll be back. Little did I know how many times he would be rehired. No, I did not say, "It ain't over 'til it's over," nor did I say, "It's deja vu all over again."

Whatever I said, however, must have worked, for he left saying he would cut down on his drinking and now he not only looked good, he appeared to feel good as well. We shook hands and that was that. A few weeks later, Reggie told me I must have done a good job and asked if I would sit in his box for the old-timers' day game. The Saturday of the old-timers' day was a beautiful sunny day and the "house that Ruth built" was jammed to the rafters. Old-timers and Hall of Famers were announced to great cheering: DiMaggio, Maris, and Mantle, and Number One Billy Martin! The rafters must still be resounding to the standing ovation that this man received; the cheering and applause lasted more than seven minutes. Fans, Yankees, and old-timers all removed their hats in appreciation, and then the announcer informed the throng that Billy would be back next season. Another ovation ensued and the fans were delirious!

Steinbrenner had scored a coup. I have witnessed ovations to opera divas and tenors at the Metropolitan Opera House and I have heard the finest symphonic orchestras of this country and overseas, and the greatest soloists in the world, but none could compare in duration and intensity to that ovation Billy Martin received that sunny day in the Bronx.

The fact that Billy and George did not get along in 1979, and Billy was fired and rehired several times, made little difference to the Yankees' fortunes during that season and in subsequent years. The important issue was that Billy returned and regained his self-confidence and won over the New York Yankees' fans who have the reputation for being the most knowledgeable in both leagues. Unfortunately, however, he did not stop his drinking, and it ultimately killed him.

All during this time, I was concentrating on my clinical practice, my work at Roosevelt Hospital, and my Friday night television program. The latter resulted in very rewarding and warm fan mail that made my efforts in this direction very satisfying. Some illustrations follow.

"Listening to your program is becoming a habit—one that is too good to change. The bad part is you don't take enough time to talk without all those phone calls. Six of us listen together now, and then talk over what you say. P.K. and the gang—men and women!"

And another one: "Just by chance, I saw your show Saturday morning. What an addition this is going to be to TV."

Two profiles drawn of a woman and a man and between them: "Man and Woman—most interesting subject in the world. You're great to talk about it on television. Don't stop!" E.M.

"In my day there were no programs like this—no TV, in fact!" U.L.

"Dear Psychology Professor: We've been needing you on TV for a long time! Good luck on your new program! Hopefully, when you're better settled, you won't get those fresh calls. Some of us really need sensible advice like you will be able to give. I live in New Jersey—work in New York. The whole New York area needs psychological help. You're going to be it! Thanks for getting started and giving your time at an hour when so many 'night owls' want to watch TV." L.H.

"I really enjoy your show and your idea of giving information and help in facing life. I am fifteen and feel that facing life is most important!" J.R.

Channel 68 was sold, and the new management changed the menu for broadcasting from the potpourri it had been to financial news coverage solely. Larry McCann moved on to bigger and better things in television and writing, and our paths crossed once again in 1981.

THE CATALYST

I concentrated on the disco and Arthur's Court but, one Friday afternoon in April 1978, I felt a sharp pain in my chest area but knew it wasn't quite like the one I felt when I diagnosed my kidney stones years earlier. This was different; this was my heart! So I walked out of the restaurant, said nothing to anyone, and walked to the emergency room of the New York Hospital which was only about six blocks away. I was right again—it was a myocardial infarct! I was in the hospital for a week, then back seeing patients, clients, and customers. I haven't bothered it and it hasn't bothered me. Hernia, lower back pains, kidney stones, and heart condition have all been treated similarly: with respect, medication, and accommodation. In short, I live with the condition and control it; it does not control me, my life, or my psyche...not even my body.

The disco craze began to die out and we were offered a good price to sell our lease on Forty-Eighth Street, so we did. Arthur's Court was also sold in 1979, and Art Heyman and I went our separate ways. *Tempus fugit!*

Early in 1981, I was asked to participate in an interesting, innovative experiment. I was asked if I would be interviewed, along with a professional guest, once a week and talk on any "topic of psychological interest." What made this request unusual was that it came from a proprietor of a romantic midtown restaurant. He wanted a crew to set up lights and television cameras each Wednesday evening and televise right from the restaurant. I would be seated at a table along with my professional guest and the interviewer would be my old friend, Larry McCann, of my last television show. This was an offer I could not refuse; an opportunity to reach hundreds of thousands of television viewers and "spread the gospel," as it were.

Some critical acclaim can be gleaned from the following newspaper release.

"'THE PEOPLE'S PSYCHOLOGIST SHOW' BREAKS GROUND —AND BREAD: Restaurant Is Studio For New Cable Series.

"Although 'The People's Psychologist Show' isn't the first program to be produced on location, it is the first to break ground where it breaks bread. At Les Petites Gourmandes—a posh French restaurant on New York's East Side—Dr. Arthur Weider, an assistant clinical professor of Medical Psychology, discusses family, relations, love, sex, alcoholism, stress, drugs; all the bewildering psychological phenomena of everyday life.

"If the location is unique for a show dealing with psychology, it does not seem unlikely to the ebullient people's psychologist of the program's title. 'Most of the problems in my house have always been settled around the dinner table,' says Dr. Weider, who was educated in the 'First we'll eat, then we'll talk' school of psychology. He seriously sees a connection between eating well and feeling well. Dr. Weider, who is also a member of the Department of

Psychiatry, College of Physicians and Surgeons at Columbia University, and has published four books and fifty articles, is a frequent guest on radio and television programs. 'The People's Psychologist' is the first program of his own, and the first program of its kind on cable.

"The host of this unusual half-hour weekly show is Larry McCann, whose face and voice are familiar to television and radio audiences in New York, where he has been a popular personality for fifteen years. Currently on-camera spokesman for major corporations, McCann has been a DJ and news reporter for WPIX Channel 11, and brings his news-gathering skills to the table for exploratory sessions into the realm of human health and well being.

"At dinner in Les Petites Gourmandes, Dr. Weider and McCann have so far discussed *Winning and Losing,* with Professor Marsha Shulman of the State University of New York, and *Coping With The Changes In Our Lives,* with Dr. Ann Viviano, assistant professor of psychology at Pace University. Other conversations include those with a dry alcoholic; a re-evaluation of urban woman's role, and a candid primer on *Finding A Lover In New York.* Guests dining at Les Petites Gourmandes during the taping are invited to join in the discussion, creating an on-camera exchange that characterizes both Dr. Weider and his show as 'The People's Psychologist.'

"'Clinical psychology sounds so...clinical, so institutional,' says Dr. Weider, who notes that it is merely direct observation of our behavior. Broadcasters have long since taken this study out of the clinics; now 'narrowcasting' takes it out of the television studios as well. Dr. Weider's supper-psychology program is a potpourri of everyday conundrums that are of immediate interest and concern the lives of ordinary people. He brings to 'The People's Psychologist Show' a professional knowledge and personal involvement that combine to produce a program both enlightening and entertaining. Information, not advice, that is presented in a simple, straightforward way, in a congenial ambience, is also quite easy to digest...no pun intended. Other topics to be covered are: teenage suicide, gambling, cancer and emotions, holiday blues, phobias, drug abuse, etc."

The B'nai B'rith College and Career Counseling office was opened in New York City in 1961, and I was appointed chief psychologist. Thirty years later when it closed, I was still on board. I had written all of the 21,236 psychoeducational reports in counseling high school and college students toward careers in diverse professions. Our longevity attests to our success. I was honored one memorable afternoon and given a beautiful modern Menorah with a plaque that reads:

THE CATALYST

WITH APPRECIATIVE RECOGNITION
TO
ARTHUR WEIDER
ON HIS 25th ANNIVERSARY WITH B'NAI B'RITH INTERNATIONAL
CHANUKAH 5747   DECEMBER, 1986

On another, much earlier occasion, I was honored by a fifteen-year-old client who, while in our waiting room, composed the following poem in perfect calligraphy. This has been framed and hangs today on a wall in my office.

> MY FIRST TRIP TO A PSYCHOLOGIST
> Quivering and shaking, I opened the door.
> My feet seemed unsteady on the floor.
> I got inside and sat down in a chair,
> The room was stuffy—I wanted some air.
> Talk about yourself, was all he said.
> I told him everything that came to my head.
> You have a creative mind, a high I.Q.
> But I wish you'd decide what you're going to do.
> I suddenly realized this wasn't so bad.
> It was fun—I couldn't stay mad.
> My troubled mind seemed ten times lighter;
> He's one swell guy, that Dr. Weider!

Throughout the decades, during which I have been a perennial student, I have collected *bons mots* or dared to frame some of my own by which I have lived, and endeavored to pass some on to my students, clients, and patients. Some of these follow.

> My definition of a typical American family is an "autocracy ruled by its sickest member."
>
> Some people who use excessive makeup are "superfacial."
>
> The difference between a schlemiel (clutz) and a schlimazel (luckless): the schlemiel is forever spilling hot chicken soup on the schlimazel.
>
> No good deed goes unpunished.
>
> A society that values things over people eventually respects neither.
>
> Life can only be understood backwards, but it must be lived forwards.
>
> A wise man once said: "All that is necessary for the triumph of evil is for enough good men to do nothing."
>
> Socrates has said: "Treat a boy like a man and he'll behave like one; treat a man like a boy and he'll behave like a boy."
>
> Winners are made, not born.

THE CATALYST

A neurotic builds castles in the air, a psychotic lives in them, and the therapist collects rent from both.

How one can tell the difference between a psychiatrist and a psychologist: when an attractive woman enters the room, the psychiatrist looks at the men who do not look at her, while the psychologist looks at the men who do.

A motorcycle enthusiast is a psychlepath.

A fanatic is a person who can't change his mind and won't change the subject.

A person who gets on one's nerves is an obsessive-repulsive personality.

A psychiatrist practices psychotherapy without a Ph.D.

Sexual complaints can be viewed as mind over mattress.

The three magic words: "You are God."

A psychiatrist encounters another in an elevator and asks, "How are you?" The latter replies to himself: "I wonder what he meant by that!"

Behind every successful husband is often a surprised wife.

My shingle reads, "Come In And Have Your Faith Lifted."

Another one reads, "Satisfaction Guaranteed Or Your Mania Returned."

"God grant me the serenity to accept the things I cannot change, courage to change the things I can, and wisdom always to know the difference..." (anonymous)

Throughout my career I endeavored to instill in my patients a *Weider Weltanschauung*.

My epitaph: "WHILE HE LIVED...HE CARED."

PART II

GIVING SOMETHING BACK

Toward the end of the decade, I was dismayed with the growth and extent of the drug abuse scourge and was compelled to try to do my bit about this condition that afflicted our teenage population. What follows is the distillation of my thoughts, concepts and energies. I founded a comprehensive, innovative, preventative program; an antidote to drug abuse. The organization, entitled Kids for USA, a club for kids only, is free to all kids between the ages four and ten.

From time immemorial, we have been raised on the premise that, "An ounce of prevention is worth a pound of cure." Indeed, a whole specialty in medicine is the one of Preventive Medicine. Surely it is a truism that it is easier to prevent than to cure diseases. So, too, in human behavioral sciences, it is true that it is cost-effective, not only in terms of money, but in human misery, that preventing the ravages of drugs and its effects on the body, mind, soul, country, and society—prevention should be our nation's number-one concern for the '90s.

The process of infusing our children with the old fashioned virtues of love of self, family, neighbors, peers, teachers, police officers, elected officials, and countrymen must be re-discovered! Our sense of values and respect for parents, teachers, and clergy must be re-awakened! Our sense of fair play, cooperation, and team spirit are ethics that can be learned as children—and only as children can learn—early, at their play—not necessarily structured, supervised play, but truly—free play. Today's teenagers and older youth, I am afraid, are a lost generation. These youngsters without hope and help are lost to drugs as their escape. The group still to be salvaged are the Head Start to ten-year-olds. This group can be reached by education embracing prevention, and one of the antidotes is Kids for USA, a club for kids only...a new system for instilling old American values through a culture of childhood with an enriched diet devoted to resolving frustration, rather than through the self-medicated way of escaping through drugs!

It was extremely encouraging to learn that President Bush was on the same wavelength, as witnessed by the following excerpt:

"We'll do what it takes to invest in America's future...the money is there...it's there for research and development, R and D, a record high...at the education summit, the governors and I agreed to look for ways to help make sure that our kids are ready to learn the very first day they walk into the classroom...I have committed an extra half a billion dollars, for something near and dear to all of us: Head

THE CATALYST

Start...education is the one investment that means more for our future, because it means the most for our children...every school and every child in America must be drug-free...we must all pass along the values we learned as children, that's how we sustain the State of the Union...every effort is important..."

President George W. Bush
State of the Union Message
(*New York Times*, 2/1/90)

HOW THE KIDS FOR USA CLUB WORKS

Kids for USA is an innovative, original way of involving all kids between the ages four and ten in a free-for-kids-only program. A computer base is kept of all kids who phone a country-wide 800 number. The youngster merely gives his name, address, city and state, and birthdate.

A plastic ID card with name and address, with the Kids for USA logo on one side, and on the reverse side, the Kids for USA sponsor's logo—sponsoring the youngster's cost for all educational materials sent for as long as he is a member.

What Kids for USA does: sends each kid member the following documents:
1. A large membership certificate, laminated for wall hanging.
2. Plastic membership ID card.
3. Yearly calendar of Kids for USA events.
4. Article: "You're Really Something."
5. Kids for USA Newsletter, sent four times per year,
   written and edited by kids.
6. Kids for USA and sponsors decals.
7. Tee Shirts.
8. Kids for USA Proclamation.

KIDS FOR USA PROCLAMATION

We, the Kids for USA, hereby proclaim that:
1. We believe in ourselves—to achieve the highest level of our
   potentials in physical and mental qualities.
2. We will try to accomplish the maximum of our assets toward
   the best grades in arithmetic, reading, and writing.
3. We believe in the statement: "If at first you don't succeed, try,
   try again."
4. We are all "someone," and will treat everyone as they are
   "someone."

5. We like and love our friends and neighbors as we would hope they would like and love us.
6. We will do unto others as we hope others will do unto us.
7. We will be responsible for our actions and strive toward healthy living.
8. We will obey our parents, teachers, and adults responsible for our welfare.
9. We will respect police, fire, and school staff personnel.
10. We will honor our elected officials and hope they will honor us, Kids for USA.

CHILDREN LEARN WHAT THEY EXPERIENCE: A CARE-GIVER'S PRIMER

If a child lives with criticism, she/he learns to condemn.
If a child lives with hostility, she/he learns to fight.
If a child lives with fear, she/he learns to be apprehensive.
If a child lives with pity, she/he learns to feel sorry for herself/himself.
If a child lives with jealousy, she/he learns to feel guilty.
If a child lives with encouragement, she/he learns to be confident.
If a child lives with tolerance, she/he learns how to be patient.
If a child lives with praise, she/he learns to be appreciative.
If a child lives with acceptance, she/he learns to love.
If a child lives with approval, she/he learns to like herself/himself.
If a child lives with recognition, she/he learns it is good to have a goal.
If a child lives with fairness, she/he learns what justice is.
If a child lives with honesty, she/he learns what truth is.
If a child lives with security, she/he learns to have faith in him/her self and those about him/her.
If a child lives with friendliness, she/he learns the world is a nice place in which to live.

TWENTY STEPS TO PREVENTIVE CHILD MENTAL HYGIENE

1. The mind of the child is complex, and no adult can hope to comprehend it by virtue of his own past childhood. Only by deliberate effort can grownups appreciate the child's point of view.

2. Good physical care is only one requisite, and does not itself insure the mental security which every child needs. Wholesome growth demands an atmosphere of understanding and affection.

3. The child is a product of environment as well as heredity. Many of the traits and dispositions are due to imitation of elders or result from training which the child received at their hands.

4. Children's education is well advanced before entering school...starting in the crib. The preschool years are the most impressionable years and the period of greatest and most rapid learning.

5. Even the very young child is sensitive to the moods of those about them and may be profoundly influenced by them.

6. The practice involved in treating children alike should not hinder parents from seeing each child as a separate person with separate needs. Differences in makeup call for individual guidance and special concerns.

7. Fear, although useful as a means of preserving life in the face of danger, should not be used in child training, because its effect on the child is too far-reaching and may cripple for life. Respect is more successfully founded on love when inspired by parents who distinguish clearly between sympathetic understanding directed toward the child's best interests and indulgence or exacting devotion, which hamper the child's development.

8. What the adult calls "naughtiness" is apt to be the child's natural attempt at self-expression in conflict with the grownup's ideas of proper behavior.

9. Mere "don'ts," when they represent unreasonable denials, may even provoke misbehavior if they stimulate the child to defy and deceive. The wise parent enlists the child's interest in some substitute activity which is wholesome and absorbing.

10. Implicit obedience should never be an end in itself. When it becomes so, the real reason for obedience is obscured and the child is deprived of the opportunity to make choices and acquire self-reliance.

11. Corporal punishment is a negative measure at best and too often serves as an outlet for parental anger. Punishment of a child should be undertaken calmly. The skillful parent can prevent misbehavior to a certain extent by anticipating its causes, as, for example, fatigue and inferiority feelings. Discipline is a difficult matter and should be governed by the nature of the individual case.

12. Abstract "willpower" is a doubtful virtue. The child should be taught to choose his goals wisely and attain them in spite of obstacles. They should learn also to restrain impulses when they interfere with their own good or that of others.

13. Children should not be needlessly suppressed. They are entitled to be noticed, and for adults to disregard them is as damaging to their personalities as is making them the center of the universe.

14. Children's questions usually indicate a need to know and deserve straightforward answers. Parents who evade or ignore them forfeit the child's confidence.

15. The child does reason, even from limited knowledge. Parents should be tolerant of children's efforts and increase their understanding by means of explanations in keeping with their age.

16. Untroubled innocence is seldom preserved, and if parents would protect the child from false and secretly given information about sex, they must answer questions simply, truthfully, and without embarrassment.

17. Play is the child's business—his natural medium of development. Adults should not interfere with it needlessly—for example, by taking the child on fatiguing trips that do not interest him, or by calling him away to entertain visitors. Communication with children to learn what they want to do and which places they want to visit could help much to make peace.

18. Habits of initiative and self-reliance should be encouraged from earliest childhood so that the child may gradually acquire full independence. The teens will bring an assurance of mental and emotional maturity—the ability to think, feel, and act as an adult.

19. Parents who encourage child dependency are in reality self-seeking because they are prolonging the satisfaction that they derive from the dependency of the child and tampering with his right to grow up. The ideal parent-child relationship contains loyalty and affection, but leaves both sides free to live independently and pursue separate interests.

20. Unhealthy habits, especially in the shape of mental attitudes, persist, if neglected, long after the individual has learned to conform outwardly to the social pattern. Often they prove lifelong personality handicaps. Childhood is the time to eliminate them. **Childhood is the golden period for mental hygiene.**

KIDS FOR USA PROGRAMS

Each month—the first Sunday—are proclaimed Kids Day.

January	is Aged Awareness Day; kids visit a nearby home for the aged and exchange pleasantries with elder citizens.
February	is Homeless Awareness Day; kids go to their houses of worship to volunteer to feed meals to the homeless.
March	is Go-Fly-A-Kite Day in neighboring parks.
April	is Egg-Rolling Day.
May	is Roller Skating Day.
June	is Spring Park Cleaning Day.
July	is America Awareness Day.
August	is Baseball and Sports Day.
September	is Races and Competition Day.
October	is Leaf and Nature Awareness Day.
November	is Thanksgiving Day and visiting soup kitchens.

December   is collecting canned goods and distributing food to the poor.

KIDS FOR USA RECOGNITION DAY BY GOVERNORS:

During the month of March, each governor awards a girl and boy Kids for USA member who, during the past year, has distinguished herself/ himself for bravery, alertness, or some heroic feat. These youngsters will be sent to Washington, D.C., during each Easter weekend to partake in a press conference with notable legislators, cabinet officials, executive staff members, and, hopefully—even with the president and the first lady at the White House.

Sightseeing, picture-taking opportunities, and other awards to each of these outstanding youngsters will motivate all of their peers to try to attain similar accomplishments in succeeding years. Press (print and television) coverage back home will encourage other kids not only to join Kids for USA but to strive to keep this adage alive: "What man can conceive, man can achieve."

Thus, the cornerstone of Kids for USA is achievement, accomplishment, and awareness, wherein kids can win rewards, recognition, and respect in a healthy pursuit of success. The emphasis on these sterling qualities is subtle and almost subliminal, but nonetheless, effective and educational. These kids will have no need for drugs in the future!

Each and every child may become a Kids for USA club member at no cost. Authorities in drug abuse prevention universally cite the need for a new, positive peer pack for all America's children. Kids for USA is prepared to deliver such a modality.

Kids for USA is a club for kids only, and that means *all* kids. A major inducement to join a club for kids, run by kids, and Kids for USA in particular, is the Birthday Present Coupon Book sent two weeks before each member's birthday. This coupon book is perforated and represents each sponsor's logo gift certificate in the name of the youngster, who is invited to bring siblings or parents to restaurants, supermarkets, stores, malls, showrooms, etc., to pick up their birthday gifts and obtain reductions for those he brings along. These growth-building promotions are inducements to the sponsors, similarly. Everyone profits. Kids look forward to the mail and their birthday gifts; families shop together and stay together; and corporations earn the goodwill they so sorely need, sometimes.

The Kids for USA logo will become as familiar as the old Good Housekeeping seal of approval on products and items of yesteryear. Corporations that display the Kids for USA logo will be making a statement that they not only support this movement for kids' mental and physical health, but that they support a new workable concept in avoiding drug abuse. Institutions such as labor unions, fraternal organizations, political parties, educational institutions, and non-profit organizations could take a prominent position in displaying their support for some of the precepts underlying the Kids for USA Proclamation.

Kids for USA is rich in special promotions of great appeal and value to the child, parent, family, sponsors, and country. All promotions held throughout the year are specified on the colorful illustrated calendar each member receives free of charge in his membership packet. Many such activities not only tie into the Kids for USA national starting dates of outdoor events, but also give new promotional meaning to such traditional areas as Mother's Day, Father's Day, Halloween, and so on, through the various marketing cycles of the merchandising year.

Parents, biological and foster, in nuclear or single relationships and legal guardianships; all these folks must have a role in the war on drugs and its prevention! Kids for USA are born, raised, and evolve in some form of family unit, and it is there where the seeds for healthy relationships begin and, consequently, where prevention begins. The traditional values and respect for oneself, siblings, parents, peers, teachers, clergy, country, and general authority figures kick in, as it were, in the crib, at Head Start, playgrounds, kindergartens, settlement houses, community rooms, church basement day care centers, schools before, during, and after hours; all these environments are the settings where prevention begins and require positive reinforcements established in the many programs of Kids for USA.

THE CATALYST

INVOLVING PARENTS & GUARDIANS IN FREE ACTIVITIES
(WEATHER PERMITTING)
(SEASONAL)

Attend Minor or Major League Baseball Games

Visit Aquariums & Zoos

Attend National Basketball Games — Parades

Attend Outdoor Classical Concerts — Attend Band Concerts

PG Movies for Children — Circus

Story Telling in Libraries & Parks — Bowling Leagues

Ice Skating — Picnicking

Boat Rides & Excursions — Rowing

Attend Modern Dance Shows — Flea Markets

Attend Classical Ballet Performances — Hiking

Sightseeing Tours — Walking Tours

Visiting Municipal Buildings — Visiting Local Landmark

Galleries & Outdoor Art Shows — Visiting Museums

Attending Churches of Other Denominations — Visiting Farms or Cities

Touring TV & Radio Stations — Touring Local Courts

Touring Washington, D.C. — Touring State Capitol

CORPORATE-SPONSORED BOOK COVERS
HOW OUR CONSTITUTION WORKS
HOW OUR COURTS WORK
HOW THE UNITED NATIONS WORKS
WHAT IS AN AMERICAN
HOW AMERICA VOTES
HOW AMERICANS PLAY
HOW HOSPITALS WORK
HOW OUR UNIONS WORK
HOW AMERICANS PRAY
HOW OUR SCHOOLS WORK
DIFFERENT ETHNICS IN USA
WHY WE NEED INSURANCE
WHY WE NEED EDUCATION
HOW HOTLINES WORK

We all realize how significant role models are for our youngsters. Of late, very few of our athletes have qualified as role models because of gambling, rape, or drug abuse. Indeed, we must now fend off the impact of a notorious cartoon figure, Bart Simpson, who cavorts about as an obnoxious, disrespectful, disagreeable underachiever. Is this the role model we wish kids to identify with in the '90s? Consequently, it behooves us to single out ego ideal figures from all walks of life for our children to respect and emulate. Each county, city, or state can accumulate its own list of role models for local youngsters to admire.

ROLE MODELS FOR NEW YORK CITY KIDS FOR USA

Fernandez, Joseph; Chancellor, Board of Education	Dinkins, David; Mayor
Cuomo, Mario; Governor	Petrie, Milton; Philanthropist
Singer, Isaac Beshevis; Nobel Laureate	Tyson, Cicely; Actress
Ashe, Arthur; Tennis Player	Mohammed, Ali; Prizefighter
Jones, James Earl; Actor	Kluge, John; Philanthropist
Lang, Eugene; Philanthropist	Watts, Andre; Pianist
Mitchell, Arthur; Dance Administrator	Stern, Isaac; Violinist
Julia, Raoul; Actor	Oponte, David; Hero Who "Said No"
Papp, Joe; Theatrical Producer	Ewing, Patrick; Basketball Player
Bough, Bonin; 11-year-old UN Spokesman	Mantle, Mickey; Baseball Great
General Powell, Colin; Chairman, Joint Chiefs	DiMaggio, Joe; Baseball Great
Hayes, Helen; Actress	Tisch, Lawrence; Philanthropist

KIDS FOR USA: GOALS

To excite and expand the real culture of childhood, to make each child glory in being a child, and while doing so, to imbue each child with the reflexes of self-reliance and pride in personal achievement—qualities necessary for success and happiness as a mature adult in a world of adults.

There is national sentiment within America today that goes something like this: "Kids don't play the way they used to, and that's not good!" A national club, for, of, and by kids, free of all costs, would turn kids away from the drug culture and towards our American culture.

Parents, teachers, physical educators, child psychologists and psychiatrists, pediatricians—even businessmen, legislators, government officials, law enforcement officers, and our president—everyone concerned with children and the future of America is searching for the solutions to these dramatic an potentially tragic changes in the world of childhood.

Kids for USA dedicates its energies and creativity toward doing all it can in effecting changes in our children, country, and companies.

THE CATALYST

WHAT KIDS FOR USA SPONSORS DO:

Sponsors will consist of one corporation from each industry. Generally, such national corporations spend $25-million to $270-million annually for advertising, promotion, and related marketing activities. There are several basic motivating factors—both subtle and obvious—underlying the attractiveness and appeal of sponsoring Kids for USA. Major national corporations are currently under severe attack by critics of the "system." Corporations are generally criticized for being solely profit-oriented and, specifically, "sinners" against the needs of society and, especially, children. Kids for USA programs are a *practical* and *appealing* way to negate this indictment, to prove by action, not preaching, that such is not (or is no longer) the case.

The sponsors' annual fee of $200,000 is literally an advertising and promotion expenditure; the full amount works for them. It is not a contribution and is totally deductible as a business expense. The fee permits the sponsor to display the Kids for USA logo on all advertising and promotional materials as well as on the articles these corporations sell to the public. In addition, a sponsor's logo appears on the reverse side of 50,000 Kids for USA ID cards; and the corporation's fee defrays the cost of additional materials sent to these kids.

In a rather unique fashion, even the United States Government calls for the development of the Kids for USA sponsors as stated in the following paragraph from the 1970 White House Conference on Children, forum 15, page 250:

> "Leaders of the advertising industry should join with representatives of the mass media to develop and give exposure to a nationwide advertising campaign designed to enhance the status of all children and parents in American life to provide concrete examples of family activities and programs, and to show how such activities can be fun for both children and their parents or guardians."

While it may be a cliche "not to close the barn door after the horse has been stolen," it is not a cliche to remember that, "our children are our major resource."

Can American really afford another epidemic...no matter its form: AIDS, teenage pregnancies, juvenile violence, crime, drug addiction, alcoholism, adolescent suicides? "It" and its effects on our children must be prevented...not "cured," but prevented! Time is running out even if there is a cure. But less costly in terms of human suffering is prevention. Toward this goal we must all pull together: government, corporations, citizens, and advertisers...to help us as a nation to survive today so that our kids can survive tomorrow!

THE CATALYST

While we are all concerned with using the dynamics of communication daily, the advertising profession in particular is concerned with using the dynamics of communication on behalf of a higher order of promotion and advocacy, in order to promote those processes that provide a quality of life that is at its optimum and not its minimum, and thus, for example, to help to prevent gang drug killings not only in our major cities like New York and Los Angeles, but in our national capital, Washington, D.C., as well. Isn't it time that we put an end to the crack epidemic with its instant psychosis that causes crime, rape, murder, and general demoralization to our people? Isn't it time that we put an end to the cocaine-induced, so-called white-collar crime among many Wall Street types?

"GROWING UP DRUG FREE: A Parent's Guide To Prevention" is a notable beginning but, alas, it's only a beginning...and it requires reinforcement to be truly efficacious. The many programs of Kids for USA can help!

Knowing what we now know about polluting the water we drink and the air we breathe, knowing what we now know about the effect we as adults can produce upon children by our own behavior as well as through the misuse of communication, and communications are with us every hour of the day, every day of the year, would we not be remiss, communicators all and advertisers in particular, if we did not get behind this new, innovative, preventative method of involving our children in **Kids for USA, a club for kids only?**

In the year 2000—just a decade from now—**Kids for USA** will be teenagers. We must be able to look back and say, with the help of the advertising profession, we did something to prevent drug abuse.

We must acknowledge that the advertising profession possesses the capacity to harness communication to humanistic heights; to encourage kids to praise our corporations; to foster generations of citizens who will revel in a heritage that enables boys to develop into men, girls into women, and children into adults—all coping with reality, without resorting to drugs in order to adjust oneself to family and society.

"We have learned to live with mechanization and computers, robots, and cassettes, and we have done this without losing our soul, our physical mobility, or our ability 'just to live' as individuals, and not as ciphers in a 'National Cipher Center.' 1984 came and went, but the Spirit of '76 remained.

"We have learned how to communicate for the sake of the quality of life, and not only for the sake of 'putting a tiger in a tank.'

"We have learned that adults teach at all times children who are there at all times, even when we think that they are safely out of our sight. Indeed, they may be out of our sight, but we are always in theirs. They know us by our leavings and doings, by our comings and goings, by the things we say and don't mean, or the things we mean and don't say. We are their constant teachers."

It is so early in the life of this young concept, **Kids for USA, a club for kids only**, but we have a perspective of tomorrow, precisely because we need to have a perspective of the heritage we must create if we are to be considered successful!

"And we have learned that playing, laughing, crying, loving, feeling, touching, doing, hoping, trying, praying, must not and shall not be automated off the face of this earth."

Advertising budgets for cigarettes, beer, wine, and liquor consumes millions and millions of dollars, with much less for drug prevention. It seems that while we think about America's third century, we must also take positive steps to make sure that the golden opportunity to communicate freely does not continue to devote so much of its genius, its massive power, on the promotion of toilet bowl cleansers and other such preparations.

Is this the kind of consciousness raising that is needed in this country, in this era? History will never forgive us if we flush our future down the most sparkling sanitary facilities the world has ever seen! Not when we have had to spend hundreds of millions of dollars, nay billions, during each of the past ten years on drug therapy, which never did any good as far as preventing the need for drug therapy is concerned. It doesn't take too much wisdom to know that "an ounce of prevention is worth a pound of cure"; that proverb is right on target.

Succeeding in the development and promotion of the understanding of an intangible—ethical behavior and positive value systems—will have been given the same benefit, the same light of day, the same "prime time" that tangible things have been given. The promotion of tangible things has been so overwhelmingly lavish in this country that, when the money spent on it is written in numbers, very few of us can read it, and when it is written in words, very few of us can comprehend it. Some of that lavishness has to rub off on the promotion of positive human behavior!

If these programs of **Kids for USA** were a new snack food, cereal, mouthwash, or detergent, all researched, developed, and packaged, well over ten million dollars would now be set aside by any typical major food packager or proprietary drug company in order to position the new product properly, to get it out to the consumer by promotion, dealer incentives, advertising, sampling, and so on. Such monies are regularly set aside by such companies for such purposes. Okay, cereal company, pharmaceutical company, orange juice company, baby food company, toy company—take the hint! Be bullish on America's kids! America's kids are looking for new heroes. Be one!

"A survey of more than 300 CEOs and CEO aspirants done for the Council on Foundations, an association of 1,200 corporate, private, and community service foundations found that commitment to community service among CEOs is vibrant...Above and beyond moral obligation and concern for community well-being, the motivation behind this giving is that it makes good business sense."

The Atlantic Monthly, Supplement 1990, p.7.

WHAT IS A KID?

A kid is what we used to be and the reason for what we are.

A kid is a very little person or a somewhat bigger person,
depending on whether he or she is four or ten.

A kid is a giant or a lion or a president, if she or he believes so.

A kid is America's most important asset.

A kid is the voice behind, "Mommy, I want...," or "Daddy, will
you buy me..."

A kid is a sneaker running, a cookie eaten, a bat swinging, a ball
flying, a pair of dungarees torn.

A kid is a prospective stockholder, a future voter, potential customer for farm machinery, chemicals, cars, or household
appliances.

A kid is the reason for the future.

A kid is laughter and problems and tears and
make-believe and jokes and homework
and bubble gum.

A kid is dependence with spurts of independence.

A kid—each of the thirty-eight million—is the marketplace of
tomorrow.

WHAT IS KIDS FOR USA?

Kids for USA is a response...

A response to the national sentiment that "kids don't play the way they used to, and that's not good."

A response to the need of national companies for exclusive oppor-tunity and endless continuity in promotion.

A response to the need for understanding and friendship between big business and kids.

THE CATALYST

Kids for USA is energy...

The hop, skip, run, chase energy of kids—kids in motion, playing games, choosing sides.

To make, market, advertise, promote energy of national companies with things to sell, ideas to share.

The shopping, buying, charging, credit energy of consumers who buy from national companies for themselves, for their kids.

Kids for USA is a national movement of kids, country, and companies dedicated to mental health as a preventative against the current ravages to society—drugs, dropout, and depression.

Preventive health is the only answer to tomorrow's diseases. Today, we're both cause and effect as far as our kids are concerned, and that's an opportunity as well as an obligation, whether we're parents, teachers, advertisers, or citizens.

I AND THOU*

You and I are in a relationship which I value and want to keep.

Yet each of us is a separate person with her and his own unique needs and rights to meet those needs—in a healthy fashion.

When you are having problems meeting your needs, I will listen with genuine acceptance in order to help you find your own solutions instead of depending on mine.

I will respect your right to choose your own beliefs and develop your own healthy values, different though they may be from mine.

When your behavior interferes with what I must do to get my own needs met, I will openly and honestly tell you how your behavior affects me, hoping that you respect my needs and feelings enough to try to change the behavior that is unacceptable to me.

Also, whenever some behavior of mine is unacceptable to you, I hope you will openly and honestly tell me your feelings. I will then listen and try to change my behavior.

At those times when we find that either of us cannot change her or his behavior to meet the other's needs, let us agree that we have a conflict of needs that requires attention. Let us then agree to solve each such conflict without either of us using power or authority to try to win at the expense of the other's losing.

I respect your needs, but I also must respect my own. This is also true for you. So let us always strive to search for a solution that will be acceptable to both of us.

Your needs will be met, and so will mine. Neither will lose, both will win, mutual respect, love, and peace.

*after Martin Buber

THE CATALYST

I must share with you both a professional and a personal anguish with which I have been suffering for the past several years; an anguish caused by a busy private practice devoted to clinical psychological problems with troubled children who, among other things, gripe about their parents, who, in turn, throw up their hands in despair because they wonder "where did we go wrong?" Indeed, a typical day in the life of any psychologist is a sad thing; no, not just sad for the psychologist, but sad in the sense of what the psychologist is hearing and what can be done about what he is hearing.

As early as 8:00 every morning, and sometimes as late as 10:00 or 11:00 at night, there is an endless ballad of troubles. Inadequacies and frustrations fill my office; deep-rooted problems with serious consequences fill my mind. The travail that reveals itself in the intimate environment of any psychologist's office leads me to an unavoidable conclusion: psychologists and psychiatrists should focus more of their time, energy, and expertise on prevention, and less of their time, energy, and expertise would be needed in treating childhood drug abuse.

On a different level, one might ask how many millions are spent for therapy each year by federal, state, and private agencies for childhood drug abuse? Add to this the sum paid in fees by parents, and the toll in human impairment that we are unable to calculate but that is registered in pain and suffering and other incalculable costs, and the need for prevention becomes even more apparent.

In short, let me just say: psychology, psychiatry, social work and related mental health personnel are effective, and I do not doubt their validity in toto, but what I do doubt, and you, too, must surely doubt, is the rationale of spending millions for therapy and what amounts to practically nothing—by comparison—on prevention...especially in terms of the twenty-seven million American children under the age of ten.

Whenever one considers children and their maturation processes, one must, perforce, think of their socialization and play activities. Socialization through play is to children what living and working is to adults. Who does not remember with fond nostalgia the free-play activities of youth, racing around the block, or behind a tree in an exciting game of hide-and-seek, playing softball in a school yard or a pick-up game of baseball or basketball, a game of jacks, leapfrog, or "potse," or just playing one of those solitary outdoor games like kicking the can or not stepping on sidewalk cracks? Nowhere is there a club for kids, run by kids, for kids only. No one seems to have provided a forum for kids via a monthly newsletter where kids could communicate with other kids about items of interest to kids. At this early, impressionable age, kids could learn about our American culture; how we work, learn, vote, live, pray, socialize, heal, and succeed.

Behavioral scientists agree today that children would be better able to cope with the complexities of tomorrow if they experienced the joys of childhood via free play and the socialization offered via a club for kids, run by kids. How free play and the Kids for USA club not only enriches childhood, but ensures mental and emotional health, is the concern of this decade.

Imagine with me, if you will, a beautiful Saturday afternoon in any American suburb. The grandstands are packed with rooters who have come to witness their sons and daughters triumph according to the rules similar to those employed by adults in grown-up professional sports.

A nine-year-old hits a fly ball out to center field where an eight-year-old drops it in the blinding sun. The fielder, after fumbling, throws it to his second baseman who tags the hitter. The umpire, a grownup, playing umpire with all good intentions, calls the hitter "out" as he slides into second. Dejected by this "unfair" decision, the team at bat now walks out to take the field. Vignette closed.

Meanwhile, at a neighboring field, a bunch of kids who have "chosen up sides" for an unstructured, pick-up baseball game, sans umpire, uniforms, grandstands, and maybe even sans spectators, are involved in their game. Again, a nine-year-old belts out a ball which is dropped by a nine-year-old; the kid rounds first base, heads for second, slides, and is tagged by the second baseman. The fielder swears he "got" his man; the hitter swears he was safe! An argument ensues, a brawl maybe, perhaps even eighty pounds goes at eighty pounds. Both teams become deeply involved.

What is really happening is that two dozen kids are resolving a conflict, some vicariously, some personally, some by association and identification. On their own, all these kids are experiencing for themselves the difficulty and heartbreak, satisfaction and exhilaration of independent working through of conflicts. Small, minuscule, perhaps, but reinforced day after day, week after week, month after month—at any unstructured game, and we have children on their way to maturity for themselves—unencumbered by grown-up pressures, rules, status symbols, values, or goals, all basically related to the enhancement of a child's search for personal identity, his ego, his peer values, his development of insight into life, his life and the life of his peers. Furthermore, the resolution of conflicts here occurs without resorting to artificial highs or by drug abuse, but via good, clean fun at America's favorite pastime.

The primary preventative aspects of free play are revealed when a child plays freely. Then he is expressing his personality; he is releasing the feelings and attitudes that have been pushing to get out in the open. Free play affords the child the opportunity to "play out" his feelings and resolve frustrations, just as the individual adult "talks out" his difficulties. Free play also recreates situations in which the ego can deal with experiences through models so that the child can master reality by planning and by trial and error. Kids for USA, involved and engaged in concert with others or alone, adopts experiences making them her or his own by fitting them into their own lifestyles.

They are not changing their lifestyles in order to realize reality by taking drugs to alter their perceptions of reality; on the contrary, they are assimilating reality and resolving frustrations within societal restraints.

More specifically, free play encourages the development of self-reliance. Each child needs to prove himself and experience success at some activity. Having discovered an area of excellence, be it alone or in concert with peers, the attainment of such prowess or achievement contributes to a sense of fulfillment for the now and later period. Development of a sense of self-reliance in early years is necessary to feel comfortable with others later, and Kids for USA programs is the developing ground that helps make this possible.

Free play develops pride in personal achievement. Along with self-reliance, another worthwhile attribute of personality development that can offset the apathy of loneliness and boredom with self, is a sense of pride in personal achievement. Expertise of the adult is built upon the stones and mortar of winning and playing with peers and coming out—not necessarily a winner—but a participant, and not a loner whose credo is, "if only." Kids for USA programs reinforce the sense of belongingness and 'I am someone.' The self-fulfilling prophesy gets its start in play, where children get to know their feelings and come into contact with their aspirations to achieve. The experience of these highs are antidotes to turning on to drugs!

Investigations made into the development of pride in personal achievement through Kids for USA programs indicate that they come via the mechanism of the child first giving orders to himself and obeying them in something of a self-mastery club. Through play, and their clubs, children develop inner strength and self-mastery, which will enable them to grow into socially confident and mature adults who can easily accept the rules of the social group while maintaining individuality, say mental health specialists.

Pride in ownership and personal possessions or a club for kids only enhances the sense of healthy peer power that rubs off on the individual who belongs to the group. Self-confidence, an essential ingredient for maturity, brings magical results to the child. These games and the club are experiments in self-mastery, to prove to the child that he is capable of commanding his own activity. Thus, children learn early that, even if they cannot control the outside world, at least they can control their own actions and be responsible for the consequences. Rules are thus self-imposed and meaningful and self-regulated.

Free play inspires respect for the individual. Respect for self is the basis for respect of the individual—one's peers. We encourage healthy, positive, self-fulfillment for others if we experience success for ourselves early, as children.

The famous German poet, Schiller, in *Letters on the Aesthetic Education of Man,* called attention to the creative satisfaction that games and sports bring. "Man plays and engages in sport to give satisfaction to his creative imagination," he said. "He plays and moves and strives somehow in some way to build and create beauty."

Also, satisfaction is achieved by the fact that, when a child plays or senses belongingness to a club, he has a specific goal in mind which he is fulfilling. Children's energies have specific aims and require specific outlets. The real, perhaps the only, thing that characterizes play is the child's inner sense that she or he is doing something he or she wants to do, that he or she believes in doing and intends to do. With all the emphasis on the physical and emotional advantages that games afford, it is sometimes forgotten that, above all else, these games bring to those who play them joy and happiness. Modern educational authorities agree that play contributes tremendously to the joy of living. Also, that the importance of joy or fun in playing is becoming more recognized and could lead children toward health and away from the abuse of their bodies through the use of drugs.

Outdoor games, as all games, offer abundant opportunities for the all-around development and adjustment of children. As some authorities look at it, play of this type is the "child's response to his hereditary activity urge, and is nature's way of guaranteeing that the young organism receives some basic experience." For this reason, although the child seldom realizes it, play is serious. It is his chief business in life.

When a child is indulging in an activity like an outdoor game or taking part in a club of his choice, he is not really playing, but working toward becoming an adult. This is why children take their games and clubs seriously in a way that adults often fail to grasp. Just as play has an external goal, one by which the child hopes to attain a conscious end, so does it have this inner purpose, too: of enabling a child to develop and grow. Play is the child's vocation, and activity is part of nature's plan for growth.

Free play offers abundant opportunity and experience for social interaction and societal adjustment. Group processes which are part of Kids for USA programs and peer-power pressures begin early, even before entrance to a school. Early childhood, under free play conditions, provides the patterns of later social interaction. Sharing, team play, and orchestrated camaraderie have their beginning, not in the crib or family constellation, *per se*, but among other kids in association with kids.

There are very few factors of the child's life in which the whole personality is so clearly expressed as in his play and early associations with other kids. In this experience, the child learns to share and to submerge his own personality to that of the group. Such wholesome opportunities for social understanding and relationships are rarely satisfied in the usual environment of the home or school room because too many restraints are placed on free social intercourse. The ability to interact satisfactorily with others and to participate in sports and games has genuine social value for a child.

THE CATALYST

Easy and companionable human relationships are established and social distance is reduced to a minimum in the camaraderie of games and a kids' club. There is no better way to get acquainted than through association in play, sports, and a club from which lasting friendships frequently develop. These are important values in living which are too often overlooked. Thus, the child is trained by play, and belonging to his own club with other kids and run by kids, not merely to get along with others like himself, but to fulfill all the essentials of human life.

Free play, particularly unstructured free play in which children create their own rules and command their own activity, encourages self-discipline and self-control. These features are what educators refer to as being so important in stemming the tide of drug abuse. Children can be reached as early as four and five to develop self-discipline and self-control and learn how good it feels to keep healthy attitudes and bodies alive. In addition, the limits of one's capacities must be experienced by each child for himself. Neither siblings, parents, nor teachers can superimpose artificial adult standards on how far, nor how high, nor how wonderful it is to experience for oneself one's own body, one's own ego, one's own feeling of running against the wind, or descent from a height, nor the exhilaration in hitting a ball into a field, or being told how great his catch was on the third out. To reiterate, a club and games are experiments in self-mastery, and can prove to the child that she or he can control her or his own activity. Self-imposed rules and regulations are more desirable than adult authority superimposed regulations. Self-imposed rules and hurdling of these obstacles lead to the development of respect for self which is the basis for respect for others, later.

Free play and participation in Kids for USA club programs are most effective teaching and learning devices for a child, providing endless opportunities for rich sensory, cognitive experiences, active investigation, and first-hand discovery. Through spontaneous, inner-directed, free play and club activities, the child develops inner strength and finds his own inner resources which will enable him to grow into a socially confident and mature adult who can easily accept the rules of the group, while maintaining his own individuality and uniqueness.

Free play, games, sports, and the club benefit children emotionally as well as physically, and the evolution and advantages lie in enabling the child to learn to develop and control the use of his personality (loving, hating, thinking, being, etc.). Actually, everything a child does affects him or her psychologically. But games can give a child an involvement with others which acts as a prime essential for mental health which will offset the peer pressure that drug abuse pushes. According to psychologists, character or social personality can only be achieved through rich interaction with others, and this is what these programs of Kids for USA make possible. Another factor to consider is the effect on a child's emotional development, in that there is a release of impulse, the control of which is so important to maturity. This experience is so necessary in the development of the healthy self, responsibility, and conscience.

Free play serves as an early learning resource for constructive use of leisure time, a factor of paramount importance in America's future technocracy, when adults will be working only thirty hours a week. Games and the activities of the club contribute to the patterns of leisure-time activities gleaned during one's early years which will hold adults in good stead later. Hobbies and play for adults will be necessary, just as it is important for kids, to experience self-rewarding activities earlier. An active, fun-filled maturity precludes a senile old age, and a preventative during play can be acquired early.

Free play serves as a subliminatory activity, a positive outlet for surplus energy and aggression. Perhaps the most salient features of free play inheres in its subliminatory effects. How energy and aggression can be channeled effectively into healthy outlets rather than in anxieties, guilt, and toward self-directed hostilities—the stuff that drug abuse is made of. The prevention of defeating, neurotic attitudes can best be assuaged via these programs—wholesome group participatory activities where one can lose once but not always come away a loser, or where one can win occasionally but learn that one can also lose, but lose at a game and not lose at everything else. As many observers have noted, sports and these programs offer a natural outlet to children for their excess energy, tensions and aggressions.

When the child indulges in play, the energy is drained off that might otherwise turn inward, making him restless, tense, and sometimes even antisocial. These activities are a means whereby a child can redirect aggressions, let off steam, release tensions, and express a multitude of feelings—all in an appropriate and socially acceptable fashion. The natural high that ensues is healthy, invigorating, and ego-enhancing and no match to even trying drugs of any sort at any time, now or in the future! When a child plays, instead of attacking someone, he bangs an object or throws a ball—and does not have a temper tantrum. This draining (sublimation) of basic aggressiveness is of extreme importance in socializing him. Where there are no sublimations or substitutions, the child may antagonize other children and adults and, as a consequence of rejection and punishments, could develop resentments to self, others, and society.

Free play is a training ground for coping with competition. The development of successful fail-win attitudes and "keep trying" abilities is essential for emotional survival in an America which confronts its citizens daily with competitive situations. "If at first you don't succeed, try, try again..." Where has this adage gone? The present generations are growing up without ever having heard these wise words.

THE CATALYST

Nonetheless, it is as true today as it was in yesteryear. Free play does afford the child with an opportunity for trying, for winning, on occasion, and, perhaps, even for experiencing failure and trying again to win. But these confrontations of coping with, rather than copping out and not even trying, is what spells the difference between a loser, and a loser yesterday but a winner today.

Free play, a necessary ingredient of physical development which ranks with food and sleep, is essential if a child is to develop his musculature and physical system and provide himself with maximum opportunity for bodily growth. Energy expended in play is at the service of the ego. Free play reduces psychic tensions, which can be considered a biological function of all play. Muscular exercise seems to be a basic need of the organism and, through jumping, running, and playing, do children experience the exhilaration of coming in touch with their bodies.

Physical educators rank activity and exercise as a basic need for all human beings, and one for children as important as food or sleep. It is essential to normal growth that they run, jump, climb, bat, catch, and throw. They need to swing, sway, skip and slide. They need to bend, twist, stretch, and roll. Through movement, they grow.

Free play provides the child with a world of his own—a place where he can be his own "hero," according to his own set of values and independent of adult standards and goals, which can only provoke frustration if imposed during childhood years. Play is a chance for a child to "see" himself or herself as a "champ."

Through identification with heroes and other real kids experiencing successes at sports, kids accomplish real and imagined feats of prowess. The club affiliation and reverie in sports accomplishments results in mastery of disturbing conflicts as symbolized in the "game of life," as experienced in the games of childhood.

Lastly, but by no means unimportantly, club activities and free play contribute to a child's moral training through the experience of sharing, cooperation, give-and-take, through practice in the ethical judgment of fairness, and through the development of a personal code of honor. Most educators agree that such behavior is a force in moral upbringing.

It also helps develop such qualities as loyalty, responsibility, proper safety attitudes, fair play, courtesy, and the ability to accept defeat as well as success with some degree of equanimity. Adults often accept the results of play activity to be obvious and tangible. But the value of free play is associated with the act, not with the outcome.

Play among one's peers offers little opportunity, if any, for cheating. The sore loser is soon found out and alienated by his peers. In sum, free, unstructured play and club activities make it possible for a child to find his own "center" and to achieve self-confidence, or in the words of Yeats:

THE CATALYST

"Things fall apart; the center cannot hold;
Mere anarchy is loosed upon the world,
The blood-dimmed tide is loosed, and everywhere
The ceremony of innocence is drowned;
The best lack all conviction, while the worst
Are full of passionate intensity."

We must, in succeeding years, all strive to right the record to where "the ceremony of the innocent" is not drowned and the *best* are full of passionate intensity, while the *worst* lack all conviction.

Toward this goal, the free play of childhood must be dedicated in the future. We must conclude that individual free play and the Kids for USA, a club for kids only, by giving the child the opportunity to experience his body, to manipulate his world without constraints, can help him avoid emotional problems, work out issues, and learn about the world around him and to glory in being a child. Interaction, during these activities gives the child the opportunity to develop ideas of his own identity, peer and social roles. Thus, it could be said that we offer an antidote against the drug culture and, simultaneously, a method by which a civilized human being is evolved.

Much the same is forewarned in the following lyrics of Bob Dylan:

The Times They Are A-Changin'

-1-

"Come gather 'round people, wherever you roam,
And admit that the waters around you have grown.
And accept it that soon you'll be drenched to the bone,
If your time to you is worth savin'
Then you better start swimmin' or you'll sink like a stone,
For the times they are a-changin'!

-2-

Come writers and critics. Who prophecies with your pen
And keep your eyes wide. The chances won't come again.
And don't speak too soon for the wheel's still in spin
And there's no tellin' who that it's namin'
For the loser now will be better to win
For the times they are a-changin'.

-3-

Come senators, congressmen, please heed the call
Don't stand in the doorway. Don't block up the hall.
For he that gets hurt will be he who has stalled.
There's a battle outside and it's ragin'
It'll soon shake your windows and rattle your walls
For the times they are a-changin'.

THE CATALYST

4

Come mothers and fathers, throughout the land
And don't criticize what you can't understand.
Your sons and your daughters are beyond your command
Your old road is rapidly agin'—Please get out of the new one
If you can't lend your hand. For the times they are a-changin'.
The line it is drawn. The curse it is cast
The slow one now will later be fast.
As the present now will later be past
The order is rapidly fadin'
And the first one now, will later be last
For the times they are a-changin'!"

War between generations is nothing new. Socrates bitterly attacked youths by stating, "The children now love luxury. They have bad manners, contempt for authority, they show disrespect to their elders and love to chatter in places of exercise. They no longer rise when elders enter the room. They contradict their parents, chatter before company, gobble up dainties at the table, cross their legs and are tyrants over their teachers."

All through history, denouncing the young has been a tonic for tired blood. As "the child is the father of the man," identification with the best of ego ideals for boys to men, girls to women, is not only needed but necessary. The two ingredients required for maturing are first, a warm home with affection and love between parents and child on whom the latter can model himself and, second, opportunities to prove his competence in career and love. In recent years, it appears all this is dead in America.

What is not dead in America are discussions concerning the "generation gap." Actually, there are other gaps, too, a few of which are: energy gap, culture gap, information gap, communication gap, religious gap, morality gap, age gap, intellectual gap, racial gap, people gap, love gap, social gap, credibility gap, etc.

To teenagers, the problem boils down to, "I just can't talk to my parents. They don't even try to understand." And to Mom and Dad, it's "John just doesn't make sense. Some of his ideas are so radical!" Alas, John, Mom and Dad are all right! Communications is dead primarily because words frequently get in the way of communication. The words of John are the words of the '70s and '80s, and Mom and Dad are talking the language of the '40s and '50s.

More than likely, the warring factions are superficial, so that the teenagers tee off on adult hypocrisies of talking peace while making war and attacking a policy of do-as-I-say, not do-as-I-do. Adults, on the other hand, attack beads, hair, and attire.

THE CATALYST

With this for openers, the rest of the arguments are bound to deteriorate to name-calling, alienation, disapproval, deception, recrimination, disillusionment, and guilt. Thus, too many youngsters are withdrawing rather than warring. While flower-children went to pot, the new disease of alienation drove informed collegians into private anomie and apathy. "Children are not fighting their parents," says sociologist Edgar Z. Friedenberg (*The Vanishing Adolescent*). "They're abandoning them." And so the gap grows wider and wider.

Technological advances shrink our worlds and cultures, while the *zeitgeist* of childhood lengthen, and communication between generations diminishes or is totally nonexistent or distorted. Modern parents fail to, or are unwilling to, take Locke's advice seriously: "The sooner you treat him as a man, the sooner he will be one."

Miles of print has been set, deploring the emphasis on social adjustment of youth and the renunciation of "the establishment." The writers who come to mind in this context are: David Reisman, *The Lonely Crowd*; Jose Ortega Y Gasset, *The Revolt of the Masses*; William H. Whyte, Jr., *The Organization Man*; Erich Fromm; Aldous Huxley; Philip Wylie, *Generation of Vipers*; Jean Paul Sartre, *No Exit*; and Plato, *The Allegory of the Cave*. Some writers have shed light on a different aspect of the seemingly unconscious, unindividuated man, which gives no form whatsoever to the adolescents of the '80s. Several studies explore the process by which we mold the adolescent into a cooperative, bland, passive, simulated adult. Friedenberg suggests that the adolescent has a natural pattern of development, which is not solely physical, but primarily social.

While we encourage individual, idiosyncratic difference! Or do we? A most efficient and rapid change is taking place in the kind of adult being developed today. This change "as a weakening in the relationship between maturity on the one hand, and stability of identity on the other" is rapid. In a traditional sense, the mature person has a personality of his or her own and has adapted to his or her environment by making certain conscious compromises for his or her own needs. In the modern sense, the mature individual is one who has been forced by anxiety to accept society without compromise, and makes adjustment a moral value. But today, the youth question maturity as "selling out" to hypocrisy! Student unrest, violence on the campus, outcries of racism and antisemitism, drugs, and teenage pregnancies are evidence of dysfunction. It is the healthy teenager who rebels against authority and proclaims his independence, tending toward autonomy.

Adolescents traditionally stimulate society. Their characteristic respect for competence, their resistance to cant or hypocrisy, their spontaneity, can be a vitalizing force. Most of all, respect for the adolescent, for his personal worth, and understanding his struggle in the developmental process, should be encouraged. Only by an understanding of this process, providing enlightened direction in good faith with an emphasis on intellectual achievement, rather than submission, can we prepare a new generation for the tasks that lie before them.

Part of the generation gap is the threat to adults that the adolescent poses. What with their sexual freedom, ease of mobility, rootlessness, footlessness, and casualness few adults can enjoy. This envy is at the base of adult hostility directed toward the teenager by the "pigs," adults, cops, editors, movie makers, teachers, ad men, and politicians. So marijuana gave way to LSD, heroin, cocaine, and crack, as alcohol gave way to LSD and marijuana and crack, with sexual promiscuity and AIDS thrown in for good measure. Teenage pregnancy is epidemic and developmentally retarded and AIDS-infected babies proliferate.

Youth today enjoy greater freedom than past generations did in dress, travel, hair, speech, sex, and drugs. Even teenagers who are five or ten years younger than today's adolescents indulge in one kind of drug experience just one step less potent than the next generation. Furthermore, sex experimentation is occurring at earlier ages, with little concern for HIV infections, or dirty needles are being used for drug injections. Adolescents, as a group, seem to reject the dictum of adults: *freedom demands responsibility.*

The suicide rate for children and the death rate due to auto accidents and drug over-dosage has reached epidemic stages. Murder of parents by their young children is increasing and, in panic, some parents are having their children arrested after they find pot or LSD in their rooms. Equally destructive are those who are so worried about their own status that they hush up serious misconduct and bribe miscreants with new cars, clothes, and vacations, and even buy expensive cooperative apartments. Still others flee on vacations themselves, leaving their kids to stage monster sex and drug open-house parties which frequently end in violent deaths. Then there are swinging parents who even try pot or LSD or cocaine and even crack with their kids in order to close the generation gap, which only creates another kind of gap, all unto itself—the morality gap.

These forms of child abandonment and actual child abuse rob children of adult limits to test themselves against. As one sociologist puts it, "How can you rebel sexually against a mother who will be happy to fit you with a diaphragm at the age of fourteen or arrange for birth control pills?

"How can a kid rebel against a mother who will give you money for a fix?" asks a heroin and crack addict of thirteen.

From thoughtless repressiveness to thoughtless permissiveness too many American middle-class parents ask themselves, "What did we do wrong?"

Parents search for reasons in each other, and this, too, contributes to an even wide schism and this further alienates the adolescent. Never stopping to listen to the "victim," the child is only the symptom of a sick family constellation and, frequently, the real patient does not find his way into the therapist's office. Frequently, the age-old definition of a family fits today's family equally as well, namely: *an autocracy ruled by its sickest member.* And the sickest member may never receive help, but the most vulnerable, sensitive, and least resistant gets singled out or attempts to resolve the family's frustrations by embracing unhealthy lifestyles.

The way to be a healthy parent is to have had healthy parents, and the way to be a healthy teenager is to have healthy parents. The key to ending the generation gap is communication, without double (confused or hidden) messages. Developing an approach to intelligent listening requires, first and foremost, regular time alone with a child or teenager so that he can unburden himself. This is vital. Today, the basic family structure, or the so-called nuclear family, is fragmented. The tradition of a family experiencing each other in pleasure and even unhappiness seems to be gone. To remain emotionally healthy, children require a stable family group, and the benefits of this stability are invaluable in even the most ordinary activities; e.g., at meal times, shopping, conversations, or in traveling.

Understanding the language, movies, music, lyrics, and habits of the younger generation without giving up any of the healthy, realistic distance between parent and child is also necessary. Respect for each other's rights to "do his own thing" is a must in order to establish an open forum for discussion, re-appraisal, and dialogue. These are methods of spanning the generation gap.

The current generation gap is wider and more difficult to span than yesteryear's. In former years, social change moved at a slower pace. The media of radio, newspapers, magazines, movies, and books did not blast the human mind with such a crescendo and within view of such a tremendous audience as that reached by television and satellite. War is bad enough to read and hear about, but today we can also bear witness to actual massacres, violence, air attacks, and destruction to bodies, buildings, and war materiel. The total input and bombardment of our sensory mechanisms "blow the mind," literally and figuratively. We live at a terrific pace; the momentum is a whirlwind of instant stimulation. Our temporal sense has shrunk into minutes what used to take hours. We now can view war in all of its technicolor, gory detail while it is actually happening. Aggression and violence is so much taken for granted that we are accustomed to seeing it on our televisions, in movies, videos, magazines, and newspapers. We have become conditioned to expect and accept such inhumanity as child abuse, sex abuse, rape, murder, addictions, and war.

Our youth has grown to distrust our government since Watergate, Iran-Contra, and Iraqgate. While we can afford walks on the moon, star wars, savings and loans bailouts, deficits, and an astronomical debt that our grandchildren will have to repay, we can not afford to feed and clothe the millions of homeless, hungry, unemployed, and children in poverty. Our educational systems are turning out illiterates in the millions contributing to hopelessness, helplessness, crime, drugs, and depression.

Generations in the '90s are witnessing demoralized times which they are inheriting from their parents, who endeavored to see their children enjoy a better standard of living. Thus, we are failing and causing them to fail and the negative self-fulfilling prophecy keeps perpetuating itself in a never-ending cycle of defeat, depression, and devastation.

"Hippies, yuppies, and druggies," as well as youth who do not embrace any classificatory labels, are outspokenly anti-familial (cop-outs), anti-educational (drop-outs), anti-psychiatric (pro-paranoid), and anti-bureaucracy (radial left politically). They deplore wealth as alienating, cleanliness as neuroticism, and prefer promiscuous sex, even in this age of AIDS, to the marital practices sanctioned by society. They play Russian roulette and refuse to be rational and "square," preferring to "do their thing" believing the "trip" is a unique growing experience, and alternative lifestyles are preferable to traditional family life. Their brand of education must be relevant, they feel, as though past education created the problems we all inherited.

To be sure, college graduates are experiencing difficulties in obtaining jobs, and rewarding careers are deferred. The economic recession, for some, has ballooned into a full-size depression. Unemployment is up, bankruptcies are up, and morale is down. Confusion reigns on all fronts. The city government blames the state legislators who blame the federal government for cutting grants and services. The infrastructure is falling apart while the environment, air, and waterways are polluted. AIDS, illiteracy, drugs, racism, and lack of values are tearing at the fabric of our society, but our governments are caught up in costly expenditures for military preparedness, trade imbalances, foreign aid, and supporting economic growth abroad. To our teenagers and youth, all of this appears as gross confusion, and distrust of their elders' judgment ensues. Parents are frequently at a loss to explain this state of affairs, and a cacophony arises when the young and old go at each other with reprimands. The youth are intelligent, informed, and insistent. We are perplexed, purloined, and pilloried.

This, then, is the emotional climate in which the generation gap flourishes. Contributing to the scene and complicating matters still more is the quickening pace of social and cultural change of the past decades. Population explosion, ozone warming, emissions pollution, human ecology, urbanization, space exploration, telestar, computer technology, artificial intelligence, television satellite dishes, communications media networks, interactive entertainment centers, space walks, infrastructure, and fiber optics are terms and concepts, not only unknown decades ago, but surely not a threat to our lives as prognosticated by many dour social scientists.

THE CATALYST

The rates of social and cultural change in the past decades have been referred to as giving rise to a malady known as *future shock*. Future shock is the adaptive breakdown that even the strongest and most stable individual suffers when demands for change overwhelm his bodily defenses and mental capacities. Anxiety, bewilderment, apathy, anger, aggression, anomie, and emotional exhaustion are a few observable symptoms. Not able to cope in complex society and within the confines of the establishment, our younger people have chosen to drop out or disengage, holing up in caves and communes or on mountain tops, looking blankly at the sky, showing no emotion even when confronted by news that would shake a normal person. They may well be suffering from this last stage of over-stimulation or entropy. For other early victims of future shock, drug abuse and overdose is the end point.

But the flight from reality and absence of emotional feeling are not the only sequelae of rapid change. Much of the anxiety, irrationality, and senseless violence in today's societies may also be symptomatic. Our elders did not have to contend with future shock, economic recession, loss of jobs, demoralization, and cultural change as our youth of today know it and have to live with it to survive. Thus, the issues of concern decades ago were not so meaningful and stressful. The youth of the '90s have been paying an awful price for their existence, and their future looks bleak as they realize the mess we have made of their world. They have even less to look forward to, except the inordinate debt built up by the cold war and its aftermath. Even tomorrow is no longer promising!

Young people no longer possess the luxury to drift awhile to "find" themselves later. If a teenage girl is not "on the pill" she may "get caught," while a teenage boy who is not "together" could get hooked on drugs or unemployment. Worse still, both could get AIDS if the proper precautions are not taken during "sexploration." At no time have our youth had to traverse so many emotional and physical landmines as the youth of the '90s. To add fuel to the emotional fires that rage, they hold their elders responsible for their plight and see no reason why they should have to risk their lives and mortgage their financial futures to maintain "a stinkin' world they didn't create."

After listening intelligently for more than four decades to adolescents of all ages thirteen to sixty-three, the chronological teenagers "tell it like it is." For the most part, the generation gap is due to a lack of closeness between adults and youth, who do not appreciate what they receive, as they do not particularly like nor do they ask for what is given to them in the first place. Furthermore, they feel that they have been "brought up wrong"—not just in their opinions, but even in the opinions of their friends. The vast majority also feel that each generation has had its gaps. They believe that their parents, too, were misunderstood and that they, too, probably will not understand their own children. Those who belittle the importance of the current generation gap, add that other problems are much more important. For instance, they are more concerned with the poor quality of education, racism, poverty, crime in the streets, the deficit, recession, AIDS, homosexuality, homelessness, political corruption, illiteracy, etc. They believe that difficulties between people are a matter of individuals, not of generations. And all of these are blown up by the media.

A constant criticism that I hear from younger persons goes something like this: "They (parents or adults generally) don't listen! If we try to talk to them about a problem, they are either so involved in giving advice that they don't hear us at all or they aren't listening in the first place." It is as though there is a "duologue" going on, where two people are talking at each other on two different topics, rather than with each other on the topic the adolescent brought up, as in a dialogue.

Equally important as the failure of parents and adults to understand and communicate is a cluster of protests against the failure of parents to grant the teenager full status as a person entitled to respect and trust. Parents tend to diminish the importance of the teenager's opinion. Attention and love is also frequently lacking, so that kids rebel in order to get attention.

Another major criticism of adults by teenagers, is "their double standard, phoniness, hypocrisy, and setting a bad example: they drink, they smoke, they tell half-truths, they practice 'loose morality,' and at the same time preach to us not to do these things."

Youths accuse elders of insufficient interest in the overriding problems of our day, including poverty, racism, homelessness, dirty politics, the debt, etc. "They are more interested in their stock portfolios, Japanese luxury cars, possessions, money, economic security, social status, tax shelters, country houses, and greed."

Adults are blamed for allowing the world to get into this mess. Youth establish positive social goals: to end all wars, to cure all poverty, to stop all evils, to promote spiritual, mental and economic welfare, to reform political processes, to further peace, love, and brotherhood, and to engage in community service. The specific problems of society most frequently mentioned by youth concern unemployment, racial strife, abortion protests, poverty, AIDS, and homelessness. "...what really annoys many teenagers is the 'accepting' of views held by adults. They accept war, poverty, hunger, as unchangeable. The teenagers look at war for what it is—man killing man, senselessly. They see race riots, starvation, and homelessness...no wonder they're disgusted."

Disengagement takes the form of dropping out of school, copping out of life, taking to hard drugs, suicidal gestures, drinking and outright psychotic break with reality. "What's the point to anything, as it (the world) will end in a catastrophe soon anyway?" is the way many bright youngsters put it. We, elders, are sometimes hard-pressed to alter their distorted, depressed view.

On the other hand, many teenagers feel that the media play up only the bad and ignore the good youth. There are just a small minority of weirdos and freaks that there have always been, but, with greater publicity, they seem to be a larger group. Furthermore, "a minority group such as 'druggies,' 'yuppies,' and 'hippies' ruin the reputation of the majority of good teenagers and terrify responsible parents" is typical of another comment of youth.

Teenagers and youth of the '90s seem to be more aware of what's going on in the world than we were decades ago. This is probably attributable to their exposure to television, movies, magazines, newspapers, and other communication media. Many of these youth have voted in presidential and gubernatorial elections. Many of them know quite well what is wrong with society and feel it must be changed. They have been influenced by the absurd war in Vietnam and some even fought in the Persian Gulf war and opted for a career in the military in order to obtain a college education. Consequently, they have good reasons for their attitudes!

Despite the pessimism of the '90s many more youth were enrolled in colleges than heretofore, and more high school teenagers were graduating than had been expected. The problems facing graduates now were jobs, jobs, jobs. Few were available and many were paying only minimum wages.

An encouraging sign was the number of youngsters who availed themselves of career counseling through the application of psychological educational, interest, and personality tests. Many of the applicants sat for hours taking these objective and projective techniques in order to arrive at a reliable and valid assessment of their aptitudes and achievements. Selecting careers in this fashion was a marked improvement over what their parents did decades earlier. Thus, these youngsters were working toward a career, not merely looking for a job.

The dialogue set up between counselor and client or therapist and patient encouraged young people to work toward goals and to achieve a modicum of success. Through these methods we were able to salvage potential drop-outs and to effect an overall educational reform that gave way to relevancy in academic, formal learning settings contributing to insights into the world of work for all students.

Youngsters once again began to get engaged and trust their teachers, parents, and the establishment in that order. Few dropped out, few started with drugs, and more began to take an interest in their government by voting. A revival in American values was possible if only real heroes and leaders could be found. In many model schools there are those with ingenuity, perspicacity, and innovation who can span the generation gap and who also can see to it that it never widens to the extent that we consider youngsters tyrants, or that they consider elders the tyrants.

THE CATALYST

In a country so diversified and one which offers more different life-styles than any other, there is no reason for viewing the generation gap as insurmountable; no reason why parents and teenagers cannot learn how to fight *for* rather than *against* one another. If adolescents "drop out" and "cop out," the parents stand condemned for a failure that Americans can and must avoid if we are able to survive amicably and brace ourselves for the future shock which is inevitable.

"This is how it begins, I see. We become so depressed we don't fight anymore. We're only losing a little, we say. It could be so much worse. The soldiers are dying, the Black are dying, the children are dying. It could be so much worse. Everything must be considered in light of the political situation. No getting around it. It could be so much worse...Let's wait 'til four years from now when we can take over the Democratic party...Let's not do anything at all. It can only get worse. Let's give up. And then I walked through the crowd of smiling people. They were loving and happy, alive and free. You can't win all the time. You can't always have everything your own way. You'll be arrested. You'll be arrested, accosted, molested, tested and re-tested. You'll be beaten, you'll be jailed, you'll be thrown out of school. You'll be spanked, you'll be whipped and chained. But I am whipped. I am decapitated, dehumanized, defoliated, demented, and damned. I can't get out. You can get out. You can smile and laugh and kiss and cry. I am! I am! I am! I am! I am! I am! I am! I am! I am! I am! I am! Tonight. In this desert. In this space. I am."

YOUNG MAN, *Operation Sidewinder*
by Sam Shepard

Let us hope, therefore, that together we can all go forward and begin to establish a healthy society, the foundations of which will not be discrimination, but mutual respect; not fear, but mutual good will; not hypocrisy, but mutual trust; not war, but peace; not anxiety, but security; not uncertainty, but confidence—in the generations of the future.

Unfortunately, a new generation gap seems to be emerging, this time between "forty somethings" and "twenty somethings," as they are called in the '90s. The "baby boomers" born in the '40s to '60s today number in the seventy millions and range in age from thirty to fifty. They are displacing the old guard of politicians, corporate power-brokers, and entrenched conservatives; their dads, uncles, mentors, and tormentors.

The old guard is not likely to "go gentle into that good night" without doing battle with these "young turks," and these will resort to power plays of their own.

Working against these younger people are problems never before considered as life-threatening. Where years ago, we had to deal with syphilis and gonorrhea, today we have to contend with the scourge of AIDS; and where formerly we had to deal with the ravages of alcoholism, today we have the more insidious effects of crack cocaine and other drugs.

Decades ago, teenage pregnancies and drug-addicted children were offered therapeutic alternatives which hopeful parents supported. However, in recent years, parents and community agencies have become so demoralized, and social program budgets so drastically reduced, that little or no financial support exists for this generation's losers.

Where in the past, sadness, ennui, and anomie were apparent, today we have a marked increase in clinical depression, suicide and homicide. Indeed, the age of anxiety has given way to the age of apathy, and our society is the worse for it.

It currently seems almost unrealistic or delusional—even fantastic—to anticipate the future with the usual, necessary, human optimism. It is rather with a spirit of diffuse anxiety and dread that we all—conservatives, liberals, boomers, twenty somethings, thirty somethings, and forty somethings—await the twentieth century.

We are all facing a tremendous debt with billions in interest payments, and taxes will be higher, despite the millions who are unemployed and on unemployment insurance. Social Security payments are threatened and senior citizens look forward to anxious years instead of the security which they were promised when they were thirty something.

The current youth look at their elders and wonder why they should be supported by their taxes, when it used to be the other way around. For generations, it was the earnings of the elders that used to pay the way for youth's education, support, and security.

Depression is pervasive in the land, economic as well as clinical. Aggression and hostility is breaking out all over, in our cities, in rural areas, in our homes, and even in our entertainment. Television programming is rampant with guns and blood. One cannot attend a sports event and not see a fistfight break out in basketball, hockey, baseball, and football. In tennis, there are frequent outbursts of vulgarity toward referees. Playing according to the rules no longer is necessary. In the past, when an altercation occurred in a bar, subway, or traffic jam, the combatants might have it out with fisticuffs; today, it is more than likely that there will be a shooting in which one or the other participant will be killed, knifed, or maimed for life.

If the police are called, they, too, are in jeopardy, as no one displays any respect for the law. Handguns have proliferated at an astonishing rate, and even children, as well as teenagers, bring these weapons to schools. Children have been killed in the crossfire between gangs in warfare on the streets of our cities. Drug pushers have taken over our neighborhoods so that children, as well as our elders, fear the streets.

THE CATALYST

During the '90s, the decade of change must fill us with hope and empathy. The human spirit cannot take this malaise indefinitely. The warring factions in our politics and culture must coalesce for the good of us all and there must be a truce in our land so that we can profit from the benefits of peace. Jobs alone are not sufficient. Careers for the next century will keep us ahead of our competitors in the global economy. Thus, we need funding for education from Head Start to graduate school, including professional, trade, and vocational, as well as apprenticeship, training. Along with Head Start, we need Health Start, so that our infants are immunized early against the ravages of measles, polio, diphtheria, etc. Poverty-stricken pregnant mothers must be nurtured and counseled medically and nutritionally so that low-birth-weight babies occur with less frequency.

On the national level, college students will be encouraged to work toward their degrees, regardless of finances, as each will be required to repay half of his government loans by working in hospitals, social service agencies, police, fire, environmental control, or engineering and infrastructure activities. Thus the youth of the '90s will vote, get educated, become community involved, and contribute to their maturity and security in a manner vastly different from their thirty something relatives of the '70s and '80s.

Indeed, teenagers are being trained during an eighty-hour workshop on how to work hotlines known as "dial-an-ear," where young people tell young people their troubles. Problems range from pregnancy to HIV-positive conditions to suicidal urges, panic attacks, scholastic failures, abusive parents, affection for same-sex friends, and other relationships. The Youthline is a mix between computer-coded information and a sympathetic young ear. Information is given; advice, rarely! The essence of Youthline is to "V.E.R.B." the caller: validate feelings, explore options, respect the caller's self-determination, and build the caller's strength.

It is encouraging to witness young people becoming interested in their government, in the economy, in the environment, and in their communities. The youth of the '90s is assuming more and more responsibility for how their neighborhoods function and they are involved in the communications revolution. They are reading more books, magazines, and newspapers and they are listening to more tapes, cassettes, and compact discs than ever before. They are computer-literate as well as literate in print and numerancy. Education is on the increase. Enrollments are up and students are staying in school and college, completing their courses in numbers never before achieved. Funding from government is on the increase, and philanthropists are contributing millions to their alma maters for minority students.

These are exciting, encouraging, and optimistic times. With peace and prosperity, we should approach the next century with hope and success!

PART III

MY PROFESSIONAL LIFE

As "we don't see things as they are but as we are" the historian might study a man's years from war to war or from the armistice of World War I to the end of Desert Storm, and the physician would study the man from pediatrics to geriatrics, I would prefer that the measure of this man extends from my first reading of human behavior to my initial intervention with patients.

What I have endeavored to do in the first part of this book is to delineate the evolution of a catalytic agent and the changes that he goes through before he metamorphoses into a therapeutic change agent himself. Maturity is a process that requires living, loving, and experiencing and the crucible by which one can empathize with another is necessary to plumb from within. Intuition and insight are the fulcrums underlying successful psychotherapeutic interventions.

In the following vignettes, I attempt to relate my interactions with former patients during the past five decades and how these relationships, albeit some unorthodox, resulted in successful, for the most part, outcomes. My patients were usually offered an opportunity to choose between being happy or adjusted; fortunately, they chose well; they invariably chose to be adjusted.

They realized that being happy could be transitory or artificially induced, while being adjusted meant a more permanent, total state of wellness, psychological as well as physical—homeostatic!

TIC & DOG

Arlene was a sweet sixteen-year-old referred by my mother, who was chatting with a neighbor in the local supermarket. The latter had this nice daughter who was a freshman at Hunter College and was doing well academically but not socially. The question was put to me whether I would see her professionally, as she was practically a neighbor. I saw no reason to refuse, as I knew neither the girl in question nor her parents.

One the appointed afternoon, Arlene appeared right on time and immediately stated that she was very nervous. I tried to allay any anxieties she had about seeing a psychologist. We talked for quite some time, and she gave me a brief history of her parents, siblings, schooling, and friends.

Throughout this initial interview, Arlene exhibited a severe tic which could be described as follows: she would close her left eye, twist her face in a downward left-sided motion and equally as rapidly twist her face in a jerky fashion upward. This was a rather atypical, but nonetheless classical, tic. During the fifty minutes she was with me that afternoon, Arlene must have performed this involuntary contortion about seventy times. Not once did she mention a problem with a tic nor did she make any reference to it. Neither did I.

Arlene kept her next appointment promptly and was much less nervous this time. Her tic was present but, once again, she made no comment about it nor did she refer to it, even in passing. I began to suspect that she was defensive about something significant in her past. But, of course, I knew very little about her present, let alone about her past. I did know that she referred to herself as an "introvert" socially. Arlene was taking the typical freshman course in Psychology, and had learned some of the jargon. She remarked upon her social isolation and losing herself in her books and studies, and long hours spent in the library. One consequence of this was that she was doing very well and thinking about a career as a teacher.

What began to emerge after a dozen sessions was a mono-symptomatic syndrome in a patient who—quite typically—made no reference to the symptom, namely, the tic, and concentrated instead on the lack of a social life at college. I decided to bite the bullet and inquire about the tic.

"Oh that," she volunteered. "I have had that *habit* since I was nine years old."

"Has it been a problem?"

"Not particularly."

THE CATALYST

"Would you like to be rid of it?"

"Of course, but how?"

During the next session, I counted that Arlene's tic occurred the usual number of times, about seventy. We now talked more about *the tic* rather than about *the habit*. A fortuitous set of circumstances occurred in the next few weeks that accelerated Arlene's therapy. Her Psychology instructor at college gave a lecture on hypnosis which, naturally, all the students, including Arlene, found fascinating. In addition, she had come across the names of Freud and Janet in her supplementary readings. The latter was known for his work with hysterics and hypnosis. In this instance, a little knowledge was a good thing because, as long as Arlene was denying her symptom by calling it a habit, it was not helpful nor could we deal with it therapeutically.

Now we had a symptom that we both acknowledged, and a patient who was willing to accept responsibility for this symptom, and our task was to deal with the *tic* rather than the *habit*, and with a psychological symptom rather than social isolation. Thus, Arlene began to behave differently although her tic persisted.

With care, I broached the issue of hypnosis. Perhaps we could learn something about her past that might help us understand "what this symptom is doing for you?" By this time, Arlene had faith in therapy, hypnosis in particular, and Psychology in general. She was very suggestible and proved to be a good subject for hypnosis during some of the simple procedures to see how well she would do. I explained what would happen, what my task would be, and what she would experience and how she could cooperate. During the next session, we started by relaxing her, and she progressed immediately from stage one to stage three and four. When she awakened, she wondered when she would be put into the trance. I informed her we were finished for this session and that next time she might get into it further. Next time came, and although she looked radiant, she still had her tic. I had noticed that she did not tic while she was lying down. We talked a little about her self-concept and the improvement in her social life which had occurred since she had been going out more on weekends. She continued to do well in school—especially in Psychology and Education classes—and she was getting more optimistic, particularly about her personality.

In the ensuing sessions, Arlene was able to achieve stage five under hypnosis (the deepest level), and responded to the many suggestions I offered. On one occasion, I gave her the suggestion that she was six years old and was at her birthday party, whereupon she began to talk like a six-year-old and was very excited and happy. When I asked her why she was so happy, she informed me that her parents had given her an Irish setter puppy. She came through this age regression session with flying colors, but I noticed that her tic was occurring with greater frequency.

THE CATALYST

During the next visit, we talked about the hypnotic regression session to age six. She wondered aloud whether we could speed up the process, and I puzzled over this. By now, Arlene was hypnotized quickly, and nothing significant had occurred during the years seven, eight, and nine, when, all of a sudden, she began to squirm on the couch, and I asked her what she was seeing. At this point, she screamed out and yelled at the top of her lungs. "Watch out, Terry, you'll get hit!" With this, she wept profusely, opened her eyes, and made the tic gesture while still lying down. I awakened her from the hypnotic state she was in and reassured her that we would understand what had just occurred and try to relate this to what had happened to her as a nine-year-old. By now, she was sitting up and sobbing but she did not tic as much. When she had composed herself sufficiently, she said she was ready to leave.

In the next session, I noticed that her tic had diminished and she talked volubly about how Terry, her Irish setter, had been killed by a truck "right before my eyes. I tried hard not to see...my first tic?"

TWO NAPOLEONS

It was in the summer of my first internship, and I was eager to impress my colleagues, especially the psychiatric staff of this Upstate New York State Hospital.

One Saturday evening, after a sumptuous roasted chicken dinner served (but not prepared) by a few patients, some of us were relaxing and planning to play tennis. The dining room was clearing out of staff personnel, some of whom were bound for the movies. Leaving the room, I passed the admissions office and was summoned by the clerk who had been searching for me because the O.D. (officer of the day), a Dr. Hill, was interested in consulting with me.

Apparently, a new patient had been referred by his family, who had petitioned us to have him admitted to the hospital. The patient lived in a neighboring community, and his physician and family felt that he should be admitted as an emergency patient. It seems he was very hyperactive, boisterous, argumentative, aggressive, and "talking out of his mind," which was the way his mother had put it.

The patient was a slight, youthful-looking man of thirty-five who looked more like a man of twenty. None of the staff was as intimidated by his behavior as his family. Indeed, we felt after an initial interview, that perhaps we could put him in a holding pattern, which meant simply that we would observe him for the rest of the weekend, work him up over the next few weeks, and decide upon a treatment plan after a staff conference. This plan was agreeable to all in attendance and as I had little experience with schizophrenics, especially those with delusions of grandeur, I volunteered to work him up psychodiagnostically with my test armamentarium, *post haste.*

The next day, Sunday afternoon, I called for the patient (we shall call him Fred) and proceeded to evaluate him with some of our least-threatening test procedures, such as word associations, sentence completions, and biographical data sheets. One notable completion to the sentence "I am..." caught my eye, and my jaw dropped. Fred completed, "I am Napoleon." Fortunately, he did not notice my expression, which I tried to conceal, and we continued with several other objective and projective techniques.

The cause of my consternation was that we already had a patient on the acute service who thought he was Napoleon, and so we could certainly not house Fred on the acute service. To be sure, while he was being evaluated he

93

could remain on the admissions unit where he had spent his first night. Thereafter, his presence on the acute service would present problems for us and our two Napoleons unless we were resourceful. To a young clinical psychologist trained in the experimental method of animal and human psychology, this dilemma was both a challenge and a mandate to produce some innovative, novel hypothesis that could be tested experimentally and which would prove pragmatically effective. I began to focus on some of the specific ideations of this patient and to evaluate his psychodynamic and psychopathological test data.

After an entire week of examinations, I made my decision. In preparation for the staff conference, I armed myself with many of his verbalizations, test data, scores, and projective information.

Fred achieved an IQ of 125, which is classified as very superior intelligence on the Wechsler Adult Intelligence Scale, and which was consistent with his 3.5 grade point average from Colgate University. Unfortunately, he was an underachiever in almost every other area since graduating from college.

His parents had divorced when he was just six years old, and his mother never had a kind word for his father, who Fred said was an alcoholic and was known to beat her. His father had set up a trust fund for Fred and this helped send him to Colgate and was his sole support after college. In fact, Fred never worked, but registered for a masters degree in English Literature, which he never completed. For the most part, he spent long hours in the local library and read "anything I could get my hands on." His tastes in reading were for history, war, and biography. He led a socially isolated life. He never dated women and was considering joining the seminary when he began to complain to his mother about voices he heard emitting from the radiator. He also refused to clean his room and stopped bathing. Furthermore, he rarely left their house and was teaching himself French and conversing in this tongue to his mother, who did not understand what he was talking about. His interaction with his mother, the only other human being in his life, became strained, argumentative, and hostile.

In recent months, he had been taken to a psychiatrist who put him on medication which he refused to take and, when his behavior became more aggressive and she could not restrain him, his mother agreed to have him hospitalized.

His Rorschach was replete with references to French history, tapestries, the Tricolor, and bicorn hats. Sexual orientation confusion was evident in much of his ideation, with bizarre content and lack of responses typical of a person of his intelligence. Associations to words and parts of sentence completions all contributed to a conflicted, fragmented ego. To love he offered, "no one"; to father, "hate"; breast, "mine"; boyfriend, "wish"; penis, "mouth"; radiator, "voices"; homosexual, "me"; masturbate, "him"; and suck, "penis." Most men "are lovable"; his mind "is obsessed"; his ambition "is to be Napoleon"; and I am, "Napoleon."

I listened attentively to my colleagues during the staff conference and heard that Fred would be housed on the acute service. I submitted my oral report and quoted verbatim from his associations and completions, and recommended, in all seriousness, that the two Napoleons share the same room off the main dormitory. Surprisingly, I did not have to defend my position and my decision was accepted. Weeks later, we followed up our two Napoleons to see how they were getting on together. Much to our reward, we could not have had a more gratifying result. It seems they had worked out an amicable solution: our original patient remained Napoleon, and Fred had decided he now was Josephine!

HEATING
THE NORTH POLE

I believe it was Martin Luther, referring to Jan Hus, when he said, "Woe is the man who is right at the wrong time." Jan Hus was burned at the stake for his attempts to reform the Catholic Church's allegedly excessive tithes, circa 1414, while Martin Luther went on to lead the Protestant Reformation 100 years later.

I thought of all of this one summer evening after dinner, when I was at the tennis courts at the same Upstate New York State Hospital, watching a fine, elegant-looking elderly gentleman rolling the grass courts with great compulsion and perfectionism.

"A patient or a member of the maintenance staff?" I asked my colleague, who had joined me for a game.

"Oh, no, he's one of our more prominent patients."

"How so?" I inquired.

This opened a long discussion which I found so absorbing that I watched this man perform his chores and did not play that evening.

The history was as follows. This kindly, gray-haired gentleman, who looked like a college professor, actually *was* an ivy league professor of Architecture diagnosed as a paranoiac. A paranoiac is a patient with a rare, chronic, psychotic, delusional, major mental illness characterized by patterns of persecution. This is a highly organized, fixed, but ever-expanding systematized condition based on a single erroneous premise which is logic tight. That is, no amount of logical reasoning will succeed in getting the patient to relinquish his ideations and accept another point of view.

These patients would rather fight than give up their life's work trying to prove a concept or patent an invention. They may develop certain personality changes, becoming belligerent, bellicose, suspicious, broodingly sensitive, megalomaniacal, and obsessive.

Apparently, the Professor, as he was called here, had drawn up plans for heating the North Pole to relieve the looming population glut and allow people to live below the icy surface. No one could fault the blueprints he had prepared; his colleagues at the university found them to be perfect. It was the original premise to which they took exception, and told him so. His behavior during the subsequent months was atypical of his scholarly pursuits of the past decades. After weeks of arguments and threats, he finally came to a staff meeting with a gun and threatened several of his critics. He was subdued and admitted to a local hospital before finally coming here, many years ago. He found the outdoors pleasant and volunteered to care for the tennis courts as a kind of occupational therapy.

He was now a benign, genial, grandfatherly type of gentleman who wouldn't think of hurting a fly. None of the violence or passion was present. Our Professor was a paper tiger now, and not the young Turk he must have been some years ago.

I found him so fascinating that I began to study his case file and read about his distinguished career, both as architect and teacher. He was known to his colleagues in America and abroad for his brilliance, and had been honored by his students as their most popular teacher, in addition to having been awarded many accolades by prestigious architectural societies. He confided in me—because I would listen, I guess—that his blueprints were accurate. I displayed the respect that I felt he was due and he reciprocated in kind. By late summer, he had given up his chores at the tennis courts and concentrated on reading the current newspapers, magazines, and new books in his field. He resumed taking his medication and, before long, had petitioned the staff for his discharge. His family, delighted at his unexpected progress, would often stop by my office when they came to visit him.

The Professor's departure was not a typical discharge of a typical patient; it resembled more a retirement from a college community. Smiles were on all of the faces: his relatives, staff, nurses, physicians, and other patients. He choked up when he started to utter a few farewell remarks and could hardly get the words out. With tears in his eyes, he came over to me, hugged me and thanked me, and whispered something I shall never forget: "Never stop caring."

Now, about my Martin Luther's remark...In 1940, when the Professor was diagnosed as a paranoiac for wanting to heat the North Pole, his syndrome was classical, rare, and symptomatic of a major mental illness. In 1964, the National Aeronautics and Space Administration (NASA) obtained an appropriation of $5-million from the Congress of the United States to investigate the possibility of having astronauts live under the ocean.

The Office of Naval Research, in association with NASA, built the SEALAB habitat which was placed 205 feet beneath the surface of the Pacific Ocean at the Scripps Institution of Oceanography, La Jolla, California. Commander M. Scott Carpenter, USN, and his team of three aquanauts, spent thirty days underwater and said, "The ocean is a much more hostile environment than space."

Dr. Richard Trumbull, Research Director, Office of Naval Research during this period stated: "Science advances as much on information from false starts as from correct, fortuitous ones; this is a notable guide for others inclined to do research in the real world."

THE CATALYST

The *New York Times* editorialized: "...Until recently, the idea of men returning to the seas to live and work seemed fantasy. But increasing population and the strain it has put on the resources of the land are forcing close attention to the food reserves in the oceans and the incalculable mineral wealth under them." (*New York Times*, 9/5/65)

By then, I had lost contact with our famous Professor, who had left the state and truly retired to Vermont. I wondered whether he had read about SEALAB and the uses to which it was going to be put.

Simultaneously, I wondered whether the psychiatric establishment at that bucolic reservation upstate might, in light of this new information, revise its collective opinions about him. Although his disputatious behavior towards his skeptical colleagues would be considered aberrant in any case, the Professor certainly appears, in hindsight, "to have been right at the wrong time."

FOLIE A DEUX

One Friday evening, after dinner, we admitted a mother and daughter who turned out to be most interesting and unique in the annals of psychiatry. Both of these individuals shared the same delusional ideas and beliefs in a most remarkable fashion. So much so that some of the staff felt they were putting us on. Why, and toward what end, I wondered?

It seems that both women, and I say women, as Mrs. R was sixty years old and Ms. R was thirty-five years old, were paranoid about Mr. R. Mr. R was a professional gambler; he bet on horses and sports events, and played cards for a living. The only trouble was that he was unsuccessful at making a living. He hocked their cars and their jewelry, mortgaged their house, and was in arrears in paying bills and credit cards. He lied to them and everyone else, and he was into shylocks and the Mafia, his family complained.

What finally brought these women to the hospital was the obsession that each had developed, on her own, that Mr. R was out to kill them or have them killed. One of his last attempts to extort money was to devise a scheme whereby he would get into an automobile accident in order to collect insurance. He was planning to have his wife and daughter in the car he was driving and use them as witnesses in this "accident." They feared he would have them killed, somehow, and collect the insurance on their lives. To be sure, he was neither the beneficiary on any of the policies, nor could he escape the "accident," as he would be driving the vehicle. Nonetheless, they were terrified and intimidated. Obviously, they could not, or would not, go to the police, as he had convinced them that they were accessories to a fraud.

Both of these women were bedraggled and shabbily dressed, and looked like homeless shopping bag ladies. They were practically mute. If I put a question to one, the other answered. Frequently, one would complete the sentence of the other as though they were of one mind. They appeared demoralized, depressed, and downtrodden.

They looked relieved when they were told they would be hospitalized for evaluation on the admissions service but that they should not discuss their experiences with the psychiatric staff or aspects of the psychological tests. Each was examined with the complete psychodiagnostic test batteries independently of the other, so that there was a minimum of interaction and cross-referencing pertaining to specific items. As a matter of fact, an attempt was made to test one patient while the other was engaged in a nearby office, and then change the patient and the test to keep to a minimum any conversation.

THE CATALYST

These two women had lived such close, intimate, miserable lives in an intolerable environment to which they both reacted similarly, that, for all intents and purposes, each had embraced ideas and thoughts that were remarkably similar both in their psychology and pathology. It was amazing to see the degree of similarity, even down to their signatures. Responses to sentence completions were so remarkably similar that one could assign answers to either one without losing any validity. Even some of the responses to deeper projective items, which plumb the unconscious dynamisms and lower layers of personality structure, were remarkably similar.

To a person, they both agreed that they were terrified and benumbed by Mr. R and feared for their lives. There was some reality to their fears that were beginning to assume phobic proportions in both, simultaneously. Each related experiences with Mr. R that sounded like recorded playbacks, except that conversations were held independently and one could not be aware of the verbalizations of the other. It was uncanny, to use the vernacular.

The flattened affect, detachment, and phobic ideation were ever present in both patients, but the hallucinations and neologisms were absent, as well. Each responded to Mr. R as though she was wedded to him, and each had the same antipathy to him for the same reasons. Their interactions with Mr. R through the recent past were alike as well, even though he saw them as different people. Indeed, Ms. R never referred to Mr. R as her father, but used his first name just as her mother would. On a few occasions, Ms. R made a Freudian slip when, on the word association, she answered "father" to boyfriend. On a sentence completion of "My father," she responded, "Could be my boyfriend." Mrs. R gave similar replies to both of these items, and there was no collusion whatsoever. What's this about truth being stranger than fiction?

Days after the pschodiagnostic evaluation of both of these patients, and after their complete psychiatric workup, they were scheduled for staff conference. The Social Services Department had been trying to get in touch with Mr. R, but with little success. He had not worked, according to the reports of the two patients, so that it was not possible to check with an employer.

Efforts were made to contact him at their place of residence, but this was to no avail as well. Neighbors were singled out, but several said they had not seen Mr. R for years. The plot was thickening and there was no *corpus delicti*. I use this phrase advisedly but, at the time we were searching for Mr. R, we did not know that he had been dead—for a dozen years, to be exact.

These delusions were so ingrained in these two women for such a long time that, for them, unreality overtook their reality. Furthermore, they were being persecuted, in their minds, as though this had occurred yesterday, even though their persecutor was long since gone. It was just amazing that this had been going on for such a long period of time in two separate psyches—hence, folie a deux!

CATATONIA & HEBEPHRENIA

The medical director of the state hospital asked me to evaluate a patient who had been on the chronic ward for more than fifteen years. She was very interesting, he said, because, for the past dozen years, she had not spoken to relatives, patients, staff, nurses, nor to the psychiatrists assigned to her case. She had received several series of insulin and electric shock therapy with little, if any, positive results. She did not respond to medication, either, but fortunately, neither was she deteriorating; she just was not getting any better, year in and year out.

I studied her case record and learned that Joann, we shall call her, was a single woman of thirty-nine who had graduated from New York University as a Music major and obtained a masters degree in Music Education. She taught music in the New York City high schools, with piano her instrument of choice. The students liked her, but other teachers found her aloof, stand-offish, and a loner. Joann was an only child, raised in a very religious household where her parents attended church each and every morning, and she was expected to do the same.

Joann had attended the local parochial school and its adjoining high school. She was an outstanding student, in the upper tenth percentile. She read voraciously and was considered a bookworm, and sacrificed social activities and friends to school, academics, music, and church.

After puberty, she became more and more withdrawn and self-absorbed. She never dated young boys or men, later on. She attended church socials, but solely for the purpose of playing the piano at local concerts and fund-raising events. The piano was her only contact with society. Hers was almost a monastic life; it certainly was an introverted one.

She then started to respond to voices she, and only she, heard. Her parents began to take note and took her to their physician, who referred her to Bellevue Psychiatric Hospital. Joann was there for observation for the usual thirty days, then was referred to the Hospital Upstate, where she was diagnosed as a schizophrenic—catatonic type. Here, she stopped practicing all interaction, most notably, talking. She ate, kept herself clean, after a fashion, and attended to toilet functions. Menstruation ceased, but this is a usual diagnostic sign.

After I saw her, it became apparent that I could not even test her with any degree of cooperation or validity. Fortunately, I returned to find her at the piano, playing a Chopin étude which I recognized, and told her the number, whereupon she turned, looked at me and smiled. I was floored. She then played Beethoven's "Moonlight Sonata," and I called that one as well. She followed this with another Chopin, a Mozart piece, and another Chopin, and finally Schumann. By the time I showed her I knew all that she played, I wouldn't say we were fast friends, but I got a response from her, and that was a minor miracle. In the following weeks, I graduated to pieces of concertos and snatches of symphonies and, as I impressed her, Joann's catatonia began to give and she actually began to talk to relatives and staff. Music helped!

About the time that Joann had been admitted to the hospital, another woman of thirty-six was admitted and diagnosed as a schizophrenic—hebephrenic type, but she had deteriorated rapidly. Her illness contained features of a flat affect, hallucinations, delusions, foolish, inappropriate mannerisms, and laughter. She would speak of some morbid or sad event of the past and smile or laugh out of context. Her behavior was regressive, with ritualistic weaving back and forth when she sat in one position or when walking, with spurts of starts and stops.

Before her illness, Irene, which is what we shall call her, had been a legal secretary at a large firm devoted to corporate law. She had completed several years of college and was planning a law career after receiving her college degree, which she hoped to obtain at night. She was very conscientious, compulsive, and perfectionistic, although her coworkers in the typing pool were insubordinate, disrespectful, and lazy at their chores.

Irene could not accept this irresponsible type of behavior in herself nor in others, and this caused her to go from job to job. Thus, she did not build up any seniority and failed to get the cooperation of her superiors, partners in various law firms, to recommend her for tuition-refund plans so she could obtain her college degree at night. Finally, she gave up on this lofty goal and found herself merely in the typist pool of a lowly, small law office.

Her morale fell; she became depressed, anxious, isolated, and morose. She was finally fired and decided not to look for another job and did not leave her room. When she began to hallucinate and became delusional, she was taken to the local emergency room of the city hospital, and they hospitalized her on the psychiatric service. After the usual period of evaluation of thirty days, Irene was referred to the hospital upstate where her condition worsened quickly and she began to deteriorate, as hebephrenic patients usually do. The psychiatrist on her chronic ward suggested that I might use her in my study comparing two intelligence scales, as he felt she was quite intelligent.

One fine afternoon, I sent for Irene and she was brought to my office by the psychiatric aide, who left us alone. This turned out to be a mistake in judgment, on my part, but I had never encountered what was about to occur; not in my young career. Irene sat directly opposite me at a simple table and we conversed easily at first, in order to elicit maximum cooperation. We then moved on to the verbal parts of the scale, and I asked her about items of information, definitions of given vocabulary words, and to repeat numbers forward and backward. We were doing fine. I then stood up to start the performance scale and started with the block designs test wherein the patient has to copy a given design with four blocks in front of her. I had my stopwatch in one hand and was turning the pages of the design book with the other and putting the blocks randomly in front of her, when all of a sudden, she stood up, jumped towards me and demanded, "Kiss me, kiss me!"

"No," I pleaded, "please do this design."

Once again she lurched toward me and yelled, "Kiss me, kiss me. It will cure me," she exclaimed.

"I'm not here to cure you," I caught myself saying, and felt rather stupid, at that. Imagine, I was answering with rationality to an irrational request in an irrational patient. The whole episode was bizarre, as I found myself being chased around the table by this time, holding on to my trousers and ethics.

LOVE
IN THE WAITING ROOM

They say, "Love is made in heaven." I say, "Love is made in the waiting room, sometimes."

Paul was a twenty-five-year-old, marginally-educated civil engineer who worked for a local city water commission checking out water pressure and the like. He was a withdrawn, quiet, shy, slight young man who loved his mother and disliked his father. He rarely dated and came into therapy essentially "Because I'm neurotic and I want to do something about it." Actually, he was a bit more than neurotic, he was borderline, and schizoid at that. At best, you could say he was sweet and refreshing; at worst, you could say he was coarse and rigid.

Paul was not overly bright, but was a plugger and was able to get an associate degree from a neighboring community college. That's why I said he was marginally educated, especially for a civil engineer's grade for a county maintenance office. He lived in an Italian home, which was always warm and full of food, together with loud, back-stabbing arguments that frequently spilled over into pugilistic encounters with his two brothers, one older by a few years, the other younger by a few years. Except for a house in the country, Paul and his family remained chained to the Bronx and his large, extended family of relatives, relatives, and more relatives. Holidays were a time for rejoicing and eating, and I marveled at how slight this young man was, after listening to a run-down of how much he ate.

He was chained to his many relatives, but they all loved the arrangement, as each family, and there were four, had little summer houses adjoining each other in a compound high on a hill overlooking a lake, much like Lake Como in Lombardy, but this was in Orange County, upstate New York. I'm getting ahead in my story!

Paul would come to my office religiously, at 4:30 on Fridays and usually stay until 5:20. He would relate the meager events of the week with an almost flat affect, as very little was going on except for routine arguments with his father and brothers. There were constant bickerings, and put-downs were the order of the day and night, for that matter. Being the middle son in an Italian family of three sons is not an enviable position, and poor Paul sensed this daily. Oh, yes, he was a very sensitive young man. As a matter of fact, he considered himself neurotic because of his excessive sensitivity. He likened his skin sensitivity to the sun and to his sensitivity to remarks that would "hurt, bum, and singe" like a sunburn. He would get very dark during the summer months, despite all attempts at avoiding the sun. This, too, contributed to much of his consternation with his father, who would refuse to associate with him during the summer months when he "got black." This could have been one of the reasons for excessive antipathy, along with the fact that Paul could never do anything right nor please his father. Once again, I'm getting ahead of my story!

Paul kept a journal in which he kept notes of what had occurred during the course of the week, and notes that he "planned in writing my novel." Frequently, he would bring his journal into sessions and would read aloud. The weekly events had more substance than his "novel." Nonetheless, I would listen. I also listened when, periodically, Paul would complain about having to pay off a small mortgage on a house he and two cousins had built themselves in Orange County. The three of them had planned, designed, and built a modern, redwood, two-story, three-bedroom house on a half acre of land they had purchased. They put themselves in hock with a county bank just so that Paul could prove to his father that he could accomplish this feat.

The house was about a thousand yards down the road from his father's and uncles' houses, and overlooked lovely, man-made Beaver Dam Lake. There were lush foliage and trees behind the house all the way down to the road that circled the lake, and there was a lovely lawn in front of the house with flowers and shade trees. The house itself was lovely, but had not been rented or sold during the three years after it had been finished and put on the market. Consequently, the monthly mortgage and real estate and school taxes had to be paid by one or the other of the two cousins. I would hear about this when it came time for Paul to pay his share. The first time I inquired about the asking price, Paul said it was $20,000. About a year later, the price was put at $18,000. I recall one spring when Paul was quite upset about the taxes going up and his payment was due and he said he was now getting desperate and would try to rent it or sell it for $15,000.

I gave him many suggestions on how he could rent it, and told him to contact some of the local colleges and high schools in the area and that he should even try to put ads in the local papers and try the housing office at Stewart Air Force Base which was close by. I also told him to try the Newburgh newspapers and church bulletin boards.

"You either have it or you don't," his father kept saying, and merely reinforced Paul's sense of failure and lack of self-worth. In short, his father was undermining much of what we were trying to accomplish. Indeed, I kept saying, "It's probably the market; real estate is down, wait for the upturn in the economic picture, your turn will come." However, the seasons came and went, and poor Paul was getting more and more depressed.

THE CATALYST

Nothing was working out for him: no girlfriend, little money, mortgage payments, and no love from his father.

One Friday afternoon, I was running late in my office and, as luck would have it, I must have ushered Paul in about twenty minutes late so that he left the office at about 5:35 or 5:40, and in my waiting room encountered my next patient, Christine. I can well imagine each stumbling over the other in their haste to appear cool and not notice each other. In any case, when Chris entered, I saw that her face was a bit flushed and I did not have to make any comment because she volunteered, "How come I never saw him before?"

This innocent remark set off a chain reaction that made the Manhattan Project and the first atomic chain reaction a mere whimper. In this case, the Bronx and Queens shook with shock waves all the way up to Orange County and environs. I just listened to Christ express her interest, such as it was, as she had rarely verbalized spontaneously about any interest in young men during all the two years she was in therapy. Her initial reasons for seeing a therapist was to determine whether she should return to college or remain a secretary in a small office; and, "Do I have enough intelligence to get a guy?"

Chris was twenty-one years old, going on fourteen. She was immature hormonally, physiologically, and psychologically. The eldest of three daughters, she was raised in a strict religious home and had gone only to parochial schools in Queens and had attended Queensboro Community College for approximately one year. She led a very restricted life, and had had one date about a year ago and had absolutely no social life except for visiting relatives and seeing cousins.

She was unhappy with her parents, "who did not have the foggiest notion about how to raise kids." Chris, herself, would read current newspaper and magazine articles about child care and apply some ideas to her siblings, but no one really raised her: "I just growed like Topsy, I guess." Actually, she was a nice-looking girl, I really cannot say woman, in a plain and simple way. She was obsequious and diffident and respectful, almost to a fault. She was introverted but not withdrawn, alert but not curious, and retiring; not adventurous.

For these reasons, and many more too numerous to go into here, I was amazed at her outspokenness when she exclaimed about Paul and in the manner in which, for her, this seemed an outburst of uncontrolled emotion. The blush attests to an autonomic nervous system response as well. For Chris, this was a noteworthy experience. Nevertheless, she made no other reference to Paul during the next sessions. She continued to talk about her work activities and her general ennui there and at home. She would look forward to her summer vacations, but they consisted of going to the mountains with her mother and kid sisters and "playing nursemaid." Here she would show anger.

THE CATALYST

Chris suffered from unexpressed hostility, which resulted in migraine-like headaches, complete with nausea, vomiting, and tension. Her physician had also diagnosed a premenstrual syndrome with cyclic depression and anxiety.

As for Paul, he, too, had periodic depressive moods with anxiety, mostly associated with lack of funds to pay his expenses on "my experiment, the house." He did mention "that nice girl who was in your waiting room last week."

"What about her?" I asked.

"Do you think I could talk to her one of these days?"

"Why, toward what end?"

Paul somehow felt, "It wouldn't be right to date one of your patients and besides she may not think it proper, either." We thought about this for awhile and left it there, and went on to other issues that were pending, like his relationships with coworkers, brothers, and parents.

One Friday evening in May, something occurred that I hadn't planned on. Namely, Chris came earlier for her appointment, and when Paul left my office, they said hello to each other; nothing more. Chris then came in and immediately said, "Would I be allowed to date that guy if he asked me?"

"Are you asking for my permission?"

"I heard that patients in group therapy shouldn't date each other."

"But you two are not in group therapy. It's not my responsibility," I said.

Actually, not only did I not have any objection, but I would have liked to encourage these two dating, as each was almost a clone of the other, at least in terms of their low-key, introverted personalities and many similar interests and recreational patterns, or the lack thereof.

It came to pass that the two arranged to date each other after their sessions with me, without consulting me any further, and therefore, I could not discourage or encourage the relationship.

Weeks later, as events were moving along well for the two of them as a couple, there was some mention of their dating in sessions with me. Both seemed to agree that they were extremely happy with the other and, in fact, both were getting along much better with their parents and siblings. Chris registered for two evening courses at the local CUNY college and felt good about going to college, finally. Paul was proud that Chris enrolled and took much credit for her decision.

Meanwhile, Paul was having no luck with the house he and his cousins had built to curry favor, love, and acceptance from his father. Following his session one Friday afternoon, I asked for directions to this house in Orange County and arranged to rendezvous with him so that I could see it. It had occurred to me that perhaps I could use a country retreat for myself and my growing family of children and, at the same time, demonstrate to Paul's father, mother, siblings and extended family of grandparents, aunts, uncles, and cousins that I thought well enough of the house and Paul to buy it and take it off his hands.

The house was "just what the doctor had ordered"! It was perfect. It was modern, attractive, red wood, spacious, had three bedrooms, was nicely landscaped, had a view of a lake behind and below, and the price was right!

It took me no time to decide right then and there that I wanted this house and my family would have run me out of town if I had decided against it. We arranged to attend to all the paperwork the following Monday at the local bank in Goshen, New York, and at the county seat, where I picked up the small mortgage and Paul obtained his money and was relieved of all monthly payments thereafter.

The house was enchanting for me and the family. I not only obtained a retreat but I got an extended Italian enclave of relatives, to boot. Paul's mother was an Italian Jewish mother who insisted on "mangia, mangia" everytime she saw me and I just ate it up, no pun intended. Paul's family were very warm people and I looked forward to the summers when I would leave the city early Friday afternoon and not return until early Monday morning before the rush hour; and this was before the Palisades Interstate Parkway was "discovered" and before Orange County became a New York City suburb.

The effect of my purchasing this house and becoming an integral part of this Italio-American enclave had the anticipated effect on Paul's relatives, especially his father. Indeed, "If the doctor thought so highly of the house, and the doctor is a man of good taste and culture then, maybe, there is something to this house, after all." So, did Paul's father reason and convince the elders in this bucolic compound which so resembled Lake Como in the Lombardy village from whence they had all emerged.

Friday nights were quite different for me and my family; we would all congregate around a large round table at Paul's mother's house and sample and eat from a dozen different dishes. The food was indecent but delicious, home-cooked, and high in caloric content. After the feast, we would retire to the solarium for different wines and after-dinner cordials. We would gossip, rib one another, and exchange bits of newsworthy current events from the news of the day.

The youngsters and women would return to their respective homes and some of the men would play a little inexpensive nickel-and-dime poker. This might continue for me until about midnight or one in the morning, depending upon how well I was doing, financially. This fostered warm feelings for the next day's activities in the country.

Reciprocity was frowned upon in this society but, fortunately, Paul's parents accepted our invitation to a Metropolitan Opera performance of Madame Butterfly by Puccini which, in those days, was still sung in Italian which they understood, naturally.

THE CATALYST

All of this "gemutlichkeit" (pardon the Italian-German literary license) had little effect upon Paul, who continued his therapeutic sessions with me during the week, even though he saw me in another role on weekends. As a matter of fact, when he talked about this spontaneously, he said he enjoyed knowing that I was normal and typical and could be comfortable in many roles. He felt comfortable with me and he looked forward to when he, too, could assume the responsibility of husband and father in the future. He acknowledged the fact that he was beginning to see his father differently, too, since the selling of the house, which no longer was a divisive issue, helped to cement their relationship. He acquired the insight that the house which he had built to impress his biological father was purchased by his surrogate father, and this, in turn, did impress his biological father.

In the meantime, Chris was doing beautifully at college and was expecting two A's in her courses. Her relationship with Paul was blossoming into love, she reported to me, and she felt great about herself. She and Paul were entertaining a formal engagement at Christmastime, with a June marriage at the country compound.

Paul demonstrated the usual anxiety associated with marriage, but his depression lifted and he saw Chris as lighthearted, as well. As a matter of fact, these two patients were clinically similar when things went wrong and when things went right. In short, what I had seen originally, years earlier, was being acted out in this new, more exciting scenario. The personalities of both of these significant characters were similar in their borderline states then, and alike in their healthier, current psyches, premaritally. Either one in a different relationship might not have insured such a positive result.

The Saturday afternoon of their marriage was a most colorful scene in Saint Mary's Catholic Church in Washingtonville, New York. Chris was a beautiful bride in white gown and train a quarter of a block long, while Paul was handsome in his tuxedo. As I looked upon both of them, I was forced to admit I never saw them appear as mature as they looked walking back after their marriage ceremony.

Their reception was held on the church grounds and the food was spectacular, but the glow between parents, new in-laws, siblings, and guests was heartwarming. Sometime during the dancing, the newlyweds approached me and thanked me for being there always. This was the first time I was hugged by my patients.

HARNESSING
YOUR DREAMS

Paul was "living happily ever after" with his new bride, who became radiant with child in a matter of a very few months. Upon doctor's orders, Chris took to bed early to avoid a miscarriage.

Paul was completing his therapy when he suggested that his younger brother, Roy would like to consult with me; would I mind seeing him? "Not at all, especially since you are completing."

Roy came to see me and, of course, we had met in the country around that fabulous table overladen with Italian dishes. All this aside, Roy began to relate his history of odd jobs since dropping out of school. His current job was as a messenger for a stock brokerage firm in midtown. I should add here that Roy was under five feet tall and weighed less than 100 pounds, wet. And what, one would wonder, would Roy like to do for a career, considering these dimensions? Of course, be a jockey!

Roy's mother would have the equivalent of Jewish conniptions while, Italian mothers had "agita," when either would learn that their sons planned to become jockeys. It's curious how both the Jews and Italians were afflicted with gastrointestinal complaints and how similar both groups were in their emotional, hysterical outbursts at weddings and funerals. Indeed, there are studies in psychopathology in which delusions and hallucinations demonstrate remarkable similarities in unconscious ideation and dream content in patients of these two ethnic groups that are not found in any other two groups of patients.

"You'll get hit in the head by a horse's hoof," was the reason given to Roy by his over-solicitous, over-protective mother. "No, no, no...I won't hear of it, you'll have nothing to do with horses as long as I'm alive!"

Thus began each and every morning, while Roy was having his breakfast and getting ready to ride the subways to his meager messenger job. His father supported his mother in negating his one and only career choice.

By this time, I was an important cog in this family constellation, and when summer came, my counsel was sought at Friday dinners in the country. I walked a narrow line by listening and never, never giving advice, especially as a guest. Nonetheless, I gleaned helpful data from all parties concerned and sought out the various hidden agendas. When Monday came, I once again assumed the professional pose and used some of my recently acquired insights from the country to my consulting office.

THE CATALYST

And so it was with Roy when, one evening, he appeared for his session and I shared with him the following proposal at peace-making with his mother, specifically, and his family in general. With his permission, I would write a letter to my contacts in New Jersey and try to obtain a job as groom for Roy. This would be an entry-level job in harness racing, with standard-bred horses, not with thoroughbreds. In the former, the rider rides in a sulky. In the latter instance, the rider on the horse is a jockey. His parents objected to Roy's working with horses as a jockey. They might accept his activity with harness horses, especially since he would not work as a jockey. Roy's demeanor changed. He beamed and looked glowingly at me as though I had performed a minor miracle. "Don't give up your day job, yet!" I cautioned. Roy discussed this proposition with his mother and father, and both accepted the possibility that he might work with standard-bred horses and sulkies, which seemed so much more gentle and Americana. Besides, Roy informed them that "Doc" was trying to get him a job, and he felt it was best for him as a career rather than remaining a messenger, going nowhere. That clinched it as far as they were concerned.

Now, we were awaiting the reply from New Jersey. After two weeks, it came and it was positive. The horse-farm manager would grant Roy an interview, and he would then decide. I coached him on how to make the best possible impression. "Just tell him about your love for horses and that you could not be happy at any other job." Whatever it was, it worked. Roy got a job as groom. This also meant that he would have to achieve a higher degree of maturity, as he would finally leave the Bronx and live a dormitory life on a horse farm in bucolic New Jersey. He gave up wholesome Italian, home-cooked meals for frankfurters, potatoes, and baked beans. Best of all, he developed a sense of responsibility and discipline which he lacked as the twenty-two-year-old "bambino" who was constantly infantilized at home.

On days off, Roy kept his appointments with me and we planned his interactions with the other grooms, trainers, drivers, and managers of one of the largest and most prestigious horse farms in the east. He learned quickly and got on splendidly with all other coworkers; as a matter of fact, he began to move up the ladder and learned much about how to handle sulkies and standard-breds and was chosen as an assistant trainer, all in a few short months.

A young man of nineteen was referred to me by his mother, who had heard about me at her sisterhood. Michael N. was a sophomore at Temple University and a good student, but unsure about a career choice. His obsession was harness racing. This is too mild a statement! Michael was occupied and preoccupied with standard-bred horses, their breeding lines, racing times, and performances, all up and down the eastern coast and at specific tracks. When he went to the track, he would take along a stopwatch and time horses before their races.

Michael had been eight years old when his parents took him to the opening of the Monticello Raceway, a track at Monticello, New York. He became an avid and devoted harness-racing enthusiast from then on. He was a walking encyclopedia of harness-racing history and current information. He read the *Morning Telegraph* and the *Racing Form,* as well as the sheets from the particular raceway he was attending any specific afternoon or evening.

Just as soon as he was legally of age, he began to work at Monticello Raceway during the summer racing season, selling hotdogs and other foods at the concessions. This enabled him to gain entry long before the patrons would get in, so that he could clock the horses and obtain other bits of information about the health, stamina, and current physical and psychological findings that could be predictive variables in racing outcomes. Needless to say, Michael's knowledge of horses and his "ideé fixe" almost assumed idiot savant proportions. It should be mentioned here that Michael had an aptitude for numbers and statistics which was exceptional, but calculus was unfathomable.

Fear that Michael might develop into an underachiever caused his mother much consternation, and it was for this and other reasons that she sought out college and career counseling. Actually, Michael had been cutting classes to go to the Atlantic City Raceway outside Philadelphia when he was at Temple, and he could also be found at the Monticello Raceway when he was at home, or at Yonkers and Roosevelt Raceways when he was in the New York City area. His mother also feared that Michael might be turning into a compulsive gambler.

After an extensive clinical psychodiagnostic evaluation, I determined that Michael was a young man of very superior intelligence with excellent mathematical skills. His verbal facility was also superior, and he had excellent reading functions, including exemplary vocabulary, comprehension, and reading rate. Interest patterns were similar to bond and stockbrokers and, of course, managers of horse farms and harness-racing businessmen. I reassured his mother that Michael was by no means a compulsive gambler, but, rather, his obsession could assume an avocational hobby and that he should prepare for a business degree at college with preparation as a bond and stockbroker. The follow-up consultation between myself, his mother, and Michael was exceedingly cordial, and they were both pleased with my suggestions. Indeed, Michael felt that other issues were not dealt with, and asked for additional psychotherapeutic sessions with me, which his mother was glad to support.

Michael and I arranged for weekly sessions, either on Friday or weekends, and he kept these appointments with regularity. Grades at Temple improved considerably, and he dealt with his father's demise. His father had been a waiter and then maitre d' at the most well-known Catskill Mountain hotel. Michael was proud of his father and of his ability in handicapping horses at the Monticello Raceway on his days off from work. Unfortunately, his father had a massive heart attack while working, and died at forty-eight, when Michael was twelve years old. The man his mother married soon after was also a waiter, but was not as impressive and colorful as his father. Michael and his mother's new husband never got along and Michael could not respect him. Michael was searching for a "father surrogate," and might have found him, unconsciously, in the form of his therapist.

During the ensuing sessions with Michael, we stressed his relationship with professors and courses at Temple, especially in Business Administration, Accounting, Management, and Psychology. He talked a lot about his hobby, harness racing. In his spare time, for he was no longer cutting classes, he would travel up and down the eastern seaboard attending races.

Michael did very well in college, especially during his last year, and graduated with a job waiting for him in a small Wall Street brokerage firm. He immediately instituted a small, intimate investment club, a legal concept which was in vogue then. Each member (all friends and relatives) would invest an equal amount of money each month, and he would buy shares of stocks or bonds which he would research; much the same as he would decide which horse would win a race. He was successful at both and, as luck would have it, "Nothing succeeds like success." Soon Michael was too busy and too well adjusted to require further psychotherapy, so our relationship changed.

One early Friday afternoon in July, I was pleasantly surprised to get a phone call from Michael, inquiring whether I was planning to go to my country home. I replied in the affirmative. In that case, he suggested that I ought to come up to the Monticello Raceway, as it would be a nice evening to go to the races. I told him to call me in the country at about 6 P.M. and I would firm it up. Less than two hours later, my phone rang again, and this time it was Roy calling from New Jersey, suggesting that I come up to Monticello Raceway, as his boss was having several of their horses running and we could all meet there. I told him that something peculiar must be going on, as I had just heard from Michael who, too, invited me to the same track for different reasons.

The one-hour drive to my summer place was delightful; the classical music on WQXR was Mozart, and traffic on the Palisades Interstate Parkway at four o'clock was light. When I arrived, I relaxed, greeted my family, had my Bloody Mary, and began to listen to Berlioz's "Symphonie Fantastique." When it felt propitious, I mentioned the coincidence of both Michael and Roy calling me and inviting me to the Monticello Raceway earlier in the afternoon. Everyone knew that I had never set foot at a racetrack before and that I would go only if Roy's father and uncles would drive up, also. I called the compound and, sure enough, Roy had already called, too, and urged his father and uncles to fetch me. Michael called, and I asked where to meet him. I could get permission to go, provided that I promised that, if I won, I would use my winnings to purchase an air-conditioning unit for the living room.

With the good wishes from all members of the family, I waited for my newly-made friends to come for me and we left for the track. The conversation in the car going to Monticello was light, friendly, warm and respectful.

THE CATALYST

The mood was anticipatory—up and optimistic. All had been to a track before, either Yonkers or Monticello; I was the only virgin. Beginner's luck was definitely on my side. Besides, I am an eternal optimist; I don't accept that "the glass is half full"; I always argue, "It's *more* than half full!" Indeed, it's sometimes, overflowing.

We parked the car, paid our admission, and went to our seats, and I excused myself as I went searching for Michael. I had absolutely no problem finding him. Stopwatch in hand, along with sheets of paper and a program of the evening's races, horses and trainers, and times of past performances, Michael told me to write down a series of numbers for the first two races: the daily double, that is the number of the horse in the first race that would win along with the number of the horse in the second race that would win. Notice I didn't say, "might win"; I said, "would win!" He asked me how much I planned to bet on the daily double and, without thinking, I said "$10." He showed me which window to go to with my $10 and ask for a ticket with numbers three and five; that is, the number-three horse in the first race and the number-five horse in the second race. He also suggested the number-seven horse in the second race, but I was less convinced, so I merely put $2 on that combination.

I returned to my seat, and my cronies and the four of them asked what I had been up to and I told them I went to see a young man and related what suggestions he had made. They left to buy their tickets after studying the sheets each had purchased when we entered the track. By this time, the horses in the first race were being ushered into the gate. Over the loudspeaker blared a voice: "The horses are in the starting gate; they're off." The excitement was electrifying, and the crowd rose as one, cheering and yelling out numbers and names of horses, urging them on and on and on. After one lap around the entire track, the number-three horse took the lead and I could hear my heart pounding. My cronies began to chant: number three is going to win, you son-of-a-gun." Sure enough, number three won by a length, and I was ecstatic. "Beginner's luck," I heard over and over again. "Now, wait a minute; it ain't over, till it's over," I heard myself shout, with apologies to Yogi Berra.

I clenched the tickets for three and five and three and seven, not knowing which horse to root for in the second race, when suddenly, a bunch of numbers and prices appeared on the tote board in front of us down behind the track. My friends were only too happy to assist me in reading these numbers, as they indicated the price winners would receive for each and every daily double combination with the three-horse in the first race. Thus, three and one would pay $20 and change, three and two would pay $26 and change, and three and five would pay $219.80 for a two-dollar bet, so that I had a chance to get $1,099 for my ten-dollar bet. The three-horse and six would pay $78 and change, and three and seven (the other ticket I was holding) would pay $95 and change. Needless to say, I was hoping for the three and five combination, as it would not only pay more, but I was holding a ticket for five times a two-dollar bet.

THE CATALYST

The second race was set to begin. "They're off," blared the loudspeaker. The number-five horse was fourth around the pole and sixth after the first lap, but suddenly ran "like a bat out of hell" coming down the home stretch, to finish by a nose. We all yelled our hearts out and we were delirious to win. I say "we" because, as one man, we all wanted to experience this win. My friends had bet on daily doubles for years, maybe even decades, and never won, and I, the first time on a track, would win $1,099.00 for a ten-dollar bet. They were not only happy for me, but by association and identification, they all shared in our common excitement.

I shall never forget going down to the window where I had purchased my ticket an hour earlier and giving the clerk the ticket and $1.00 and getting back eleven $100 bills. I really had to fight getting hooked! And I did not.

We stayed for a few other races, but everything else was anticlimactic. Before leaving I sought out Michael and he couldn't get over what he had wrought! Before going home, I suggested that we celebrate by going to a restaurant on the Quickway on the way. I picked up the check gladly, but the main topic of conversation was the big win.

The family was up and waiting for news of my first horse-racing experience. We had another celebration after the shouting quieted down, and plans were made to purchase that air conditioner I had promised. Saturday afternoon, the next day after my victory, found us at a large appliance warehouse building looking at the biggest air conditioner we could carry back in our station wagon. The price was right, as it cost about $525.00, tax and all. This was about twenty-five years ago, and the machine still works, cooling not only the large living room but the entire lower level of the country house, and stands as a trophy to my first winnings.

On his own, Michael met Roy at Monticello Raceway, and they both discovered they had a mutual friend. Michael also made the acquaintance of one of my colleagues, a psychiatrist who owned and boarded more than 110 horses on a farm of 125 acres, in upstate New York about twenty miles south of the Monticello Raceway and even closer to the Hambletonian Historic Track, the oldest harness-racing track in the United States. For years, we would all congregate on July Fourth afternoon to watch the Sire Stakes (horses born and bred in New York State) in this Goshen landmark picturesque track which was open only for one week in July of each year, as the Hambletonian later moved to Illinois and back to the Meadowlands in New Jersey, recently. Dr. Berl owned several horses that were eligible to run in these Sire States, and we sat in his box and always had fun. Sometimes we even won!

In the fall of this momentous year, I received a phone call from Michael, who had been to Atlantic City Raceway and was following a horse that "had good blood lines, good race performance and winnings, and was in a claiming race." All of this meant that the horse could be and should be purchased. For no significant reason, as it brings nothing to bear on the history of the health of the horse, I asked, "What is the horse's name?"

"'Michael N.,'" said Michael N.

"Are you kidding?"

"No!"

It was Barshert, low German for "it is destined, fated," so to speak. Imagine a horse all the way from Australia with the name "Michael N."; the N means Australia, and being recommended by Michael N, my horse mentor. I obtained a certified check for $6,000, made out to Atlantic City Raceway, and hoped to claim "Michael N." Days later, I owned a horse.

Roy harnessed his dreams, Michael harnessed his dreams; now it was my turn. I merely wanted to make sure that my dreams would not turn into nightmares.

This was a foray into an avocation that could be costly and that required a license as a horseman and that required a trainer, driver, feeding and boarding fees, insurance, and lots of hidden expenses. The advantages were many, also. We could travel to local tracks and watch our horse run and, hopefully, win, and we would get into the winners' circle and have our pictures taken. The family just adored this kind of notoriety, especially the children; besides, the horse attached to the sulky was so reminiscent of Currier and Ives and a bit of Americana. Or was this my rationalization?

In any case, "Michael N," the horse, that is, ran and won more often than he lost and he made more money than he cost to maintain. We have lots of pictures of him winning by a whisker, by a nose, by a length, by two lengths, and by as many as six lengths. There are even pictures with us in the winners' circle. Furthermore, we visited Wilkes-Barre, Atlantic City Raceway, Maryland, Pocono Downs, Monticello Raceway, Yonkers Raceway, and Roosevelt Raceway. After more than three years, "Michael N" became lame and was sold to a farm in Canada. We still love him.

"Fly Fly Irene" was the next three-year-old that I purchased from Dr. Berl, who owned her sire, the famous "Fly Fly Byrd." "Fly Fly Irene" won the first six races she ran and was written up as the darling of the circuit at Monticello Raceway. She, too, earned her keep and gave us many, many pictures in the winners' circle to add to our collection, and they, too, adorn our walls.

ERROL FLYNN'S ALTER EGO

A young man of thirty-two hobbled into my office on a cane and looked almost ten years older than his stated years. He was shabbily dressed, unshaven, and looked depressed. His tale of woe unfolded easily, as he was very fluent and articulate and sounded like a man educated at a university.

John dropped out of a Bronx high school in his last year and headed to California; Los Angeles to be exact. There he experimented with drugs, graduating from marijuana to LSD and heroin. He discovered Malibu and water surfing, and excelled at the latter so much so that he developed a following and began teaching wealthy adolescents how to swim, surf, and drop out from school, responsibility, and society. He also began to abuse alcohol to the point where friends called him an alcoholic, which he denied. His popularity grew immeasurably, and his chest would swell when reference was made finding similarities between his swashbuckling demeanor and Errol Flynn's. The more he heard of this likeness, the more his ego diminished into the background and he began to adopt the stance, carriage, and walk of the then-famous actor.

He lived "the life of Riley," another Irishman of whom he was very proud. He became a surfer-bum, languishing on the beach each and every day, and refused to engage in further education toward a career. He went from job to job and could not hold onto one for more than a few weeks, due to his drinking problem. He worked in bars and was summarily fired even from these, for drinking and irresponsibility. As he could not handle jobs, his funds began to dwindle and he was forced to steal and con his so-called friends to obtain money for drugs and alcohol. After awhile, he began to push drugs to afford his digs. All along, however, he enjoyed his identification with Errol Flynn and still basked in the sunshine, getting a tan over his entire body and pumping iron to build up his physique and muscles to resemble the actor's.

He was very intelligent but undisciplined; he was very well-read, but on subjects he chose, not those required in high school literature. He was quite a debater, able to discuss Greek and Roman philosophers, but he could not carry on a discussion about practical economic matters of self-support. He was lazy, indolent, argumentative, belligerent, and quick to start a fight in which he usually conquered his unsuspecting foe. John was a violent time bomb, waiting to explode or self-destruct.

THE CATALYST

He was so full of himself, or, rather, Errol Flynn, that his ego mitigated against real personal harm, except one afternoon, so the story goes, when he was "performing" before his buddies at Malibu and had much too much LSD in him. He went to the roof of a four-story building and, with an umbrella in one hand and a hat in the other, on the order of a trapeze high-wire balancing actor, he tried to walk along the edge. He lost his balance and fell to the pavement in front of the building, to the horror and dismay of the crowd that had convened to watch this daredevil. He was taken to the local hospital, and when he regained consciousness, was told that he had fractured both legs and his pelvic girdle, and broken his back at the coccyx.

After two months at a rehabilitation center, he was discharged with a cane and he returned to New York City, literally a broken man. John was lonely and bitter, having to live in the South Bronx from whence he had fled years ago to make his mark and movie debut in Hollywood as Errol Flynn's look-alike, and now was a failure and was looking forward to welfare as a means of surviving.

With my assistance, he applied for Social Security Disability, which gave him a small monthly allowance, and I referred him for a job as a writer and researcher for a local community newspaper. He passed the intelligence test with flying colors at the newspaper, and was given a nice salary so that he gave up the Social Security Disability checks. John lacked friends in New York and, because of his noticeable limp, became an introverted, social isolate. However, he began to read extensively.

John needed surgery months after he started therapy, and the only facility where this could be arranged without charge was the medical infirmary of Creedmore State Hospital on Long Island, as many years before going to California, he had been a patient there on the alcoholic service.

With my monitoring his behavior and department at his job, John was doing nicely, according to his supervisors. He came to work on time and was not absent and, indeed, was conscientious and capable. We hoped he could get time off with pay for his surgery by working a few more months without upsetting his splendid work performance. As the months flew by, and John continued to show real progress in his behavior, he was ready for his major surgery. He requested time off. The newspaper's personnel department cooperated and gave him his three-week vacation early. I arranged to have him return to Creedmore and to the medical service for the surgery.

Mary had been a former student of mine at Bellevue Hospital School of Nursing who dropped out in her first year because of the pressure and stress of classes. She had always wanted to be a nun or a nurse and chose the latter, but found the anatomy, biochemistry, and physiology too much. She came into therapy several months ago, and we began to search for other careers and we came up with baby care. She attended a short six-month course of study for infant and baby care. I recommended her to the New York Foundling Hospital, which accepted her because of her time at Bellevue and her newly acquired expertise. She got the job and continued to see me, and what soon became obvious was her intense desire to have a child of her own, especially since she was caring for so many unloved orphans and babies left on doorsteps throughout the city.

Withdrawn, shy, and timid, Mary rarely dated and was envious of her younger sister who was better educated, more social, and already married. In our sessions, it soon became apparent that Mary would benefit when she cared for babies, pets, or a friend. As I thought about this on one occasion, it suddenly occurred to me that I might suggest to Mary that she visit John when he was hospitalized for his surgery.

I asked her to consider visiting a patient of mine who was in a hospital for orthopedic surgery and who lived alone and had no one who would visit him. I told her that I felt it would be beneficial to both of them, and perhaps they could become friends during his convalescence later. She said she would think about it and let me know during the next session. Fortunately, she decided in the affirmative, and I told her his name, where he was, and how to get there. When he learned he would have a visitor, John was delighted. Armed with a carton of cigarettes, writing paper, and a bouquet of flowers, Mary appeared at the hospital and the visit to John began. To say it was love at first sight would be a slight exaggeration. But these two souls were so desperate and needy for some emotional contact from the opposite sex that this dyad just could not miss.

When Mary was returning to the city, she had an appointment with me, and John had already called ahead to tell me how grateful he was to her and me for arranging a visit. "She's very sweet," I recall him saying. When Mary arrived, she was all aglow, beaming from ear to ear, and related how good-looking he was. He was still bed-ridden, and she could not see the mess he was on his feet, but that did not matter.

She had already planned to visit him on her next day off and was looking forward to his letter, which he had promised her. Mary kept her appointment with me and brought in two letters John had sent. At this point, she told me these were the first letters she ever received from a man other than her brothers. John's sense of humor and his ability to write well came through in his letters and he demonstrated a warm side I never knew he possessed. Mary had not yet written, as she was planning to visit him after her appointment with me. A significant byproduct of John's hospitalization was his kicking the abuse of substances, as he told me on the phone; "No more booze, LSD, roaches, and even cigarettes." Consequently, I told Mary no more cigarettes; flowers were all right. At this point, I still felt a bit uncomfortable, as John was lightyears ahead of Mary in experience, maturity, and street smarts; could she catch up?

THE CATALYST

Not only did Mary catch up, but she demonstrated a resiliency and strength of purpose that I never saw in therapy. She was determined to cure him. "Cure him of what?" I asked. Mary ran down several aspects of his psyche that I did not think would be so apparent so soon, but she had been alerted quickly and correctly. John opened up to her quickly because he had so much to say to a woman, as there were so few he could trust in his past. John sensed that Mary could be real and down-to-earth, and was trustworthy.

John kept in touch with me by phone all during the six weeks of his hospitalization, and I was able to detect real progress in his attitude about himself, his psychopathology, and his relationship with Mary. He was looking forward to getting out of the hospital, even though he did not know yet how he would be able to walk. He was anxious to get back to work after being away so long, and I was able to obtain a longer medical leave for him. Above all, he felt "like a man," now that he had a woman who was interested in him. In this connection, Mary felt "like a woman," now that she had a man who was interested in her. With some slight trepidation, I encouraged this relationship and allowed it to continue.

Now Mary was visiting John not only on her days off from the Foundling Home where she worked full-time, but would make the long trek on weekends, too. John just basked in all of this attention and beamed when he introduced her to the other patients, staff, and doctors as his girlfriend. As for Mary, she loved every minute of it, too, and it was noticeable to me, her siblings, and her mother that Mary was falling in love, and no one thought this was happening too fast.

Mary had prevailed upon her mother, who had visited John in the hospital, to allow him to move into Mary's room, while she would move into the smaller guest room they had. Both would go downtown by subway to work each morning and meet for the return trip back. On several occasions, they would meet in my office when either he or she had their appointments with me. By this time, John was able to get around easily and soon gave up his cane. All during this time, he never mentioned Errol Flynn either to me or Mary; apparently his own identity was sufficient for his ego now that he was getting whole again, or perhaps, for the first time.

His progress at the newspaper was steady and he was getting periodic raises, and Mary, too, was doing better financially at the Foundling Hospital. A few months later, both arranged to see me as a couple and announced their engagement. Early in June, we all congregated in one of the most beautiful Catholic churches in the West Bronx for a wedding ceremony that was notable in that this was the first Saturday after the council of bishops permitted the ceremony to be spoken in the vernacular rather than in the usual Latin. Thus, it was possible to understand the wedding ceremony and to hear almost every other word: "Israel" and "Hear, oh Children of Israel."

THE CATALYST

Mary looked like the Madonna herself when she held her firstborn daughter, and I shall never forget how thankful to me she was when I visited her in Staten Island where they decided to move. I often hear from this little family I put together, as they now have three lovely children and they are all so very happy. I would do it again!

GODFATHER
TO AN ADOPTION

An obstetrician-gynecologist referred a woman to me for depression. Lucy came to my office in Manhasset, Long Island, on the Miracle Mile. She claimed to weigh about 275 pounds, but she appeared to weigh much more. Her chief source for depression was being turned down by all legal adoption agencies in the State of New York, in general, and New York City in particular.

She kept her appointments religiously, as we covered all aspects of her childhood, adolescence, menses, premarital sex life, and her marriage to a very fine, conscientious man. Lucy had been a secretary, and her husband owned a hardware store with is brother. For years, they had been trying to have a child of their own, but without success. They had literally tried every available option suggested by their world-renowned ob-gyn specialist, who referred them to me.

Ken weighed 280 pounds, so he said, but also appeared to weigh more than 300 pounds. I might add that both of these two lovely people were just a bit over five feet tall. Ostensibly, they were turned down by adoption agencies because of their weight problems and the effect of this on their hearts, blood pressure, and circulation.

While Lucy was clinically depressed, Ken was hurt, humiliated, and angry at himself and his brother and the many agencies who "turned us away without even interviewing us. We would have given everything we have to get a little girl."

There were three topics that Lucy would talk about without embarrassment. These were: adopting a daughter, food, and sex. As for the latter, she disclosed that she and her husband actually had difficulty performing normal intercourse, essentially due to their girth. Her physician lectured them on different techniques that could be utilized to overcome this obstacle. However, they did not meet with much success most of the time. Nonetheless, they were warm and in love even more now than when they first married. Lucy and Ken were not only devoted to each other, but to their families, as well, and most of their social lives revolved around their parents, siblings, and nieces and nephews; theirs was a large extended family. Holidays were always feasts, and obesity was the norm among all of them.

Lucy's depression was caused by an obsession about having a baby or adopting a baby and not being able to do anything about it. In addition,

THE CATALYST

little hope was being held out to her, and this anger was being turned inward. On the surface, she claimed not to be angry with Ken, but I felt she declared this much too much, and she was certainly angry with his brother, who was his partner. This brother was thin, muscular, an in-charge kind of a man with three lovely children and a svelte, thin wife; "They had everything." Mockingly, Lucy once remarked that as his brother could make nice babies, "Why couldn't he make one for us, he just about does everything else for us...he's so much in-charge." At this, she burst into tears and sobbed profusely.

Lucy came to my office and announced that she was getting desperate. "What does that mean?" I inquired gingerly.

"We may have to go illegal."

"Explain further."

"Well, there are lawyers and doctors where we could "buy" a baby."

"Lucy, you don't want to do that, you shouldn't have to do that. You've been so patient, why not wait a bit longer? Besides, there is no biological clock ticking."

Our sessions were getting tougher and tougher for both of us. Lucy was beginning to lose hope, and her depressions were getting longer and were being sustained and dark. Fortunately, she never verbalized suicide and I discarded this as a possibility, not because she was so narcissistic but because she was somewhat religious and wouldn't want to hurt her family.

During one session in the middle of August (unlike most of my colleagues, I was not on vacation), I tried to give Lucy hope and said the following: "Lucy, although it is now August 18th, I promise you that before the end of this year you will become a mother! I just know it. Don't ask me how; just have faith."

Something must have happened during that session. Lucy went home and returned. Labor Day came and went. Holy days and holidays came and went, and Lucy's depression wasn't cured, but it began to lift.

One evening after our session, during the first snowstorm of the winter season, I asked her how she was getting home, and she said, "By bus."

"I'll give you a lift, as it's on my way back to New York."

"Fine, in return, I'll give you a slice of my homemade cheesecake."

We parked the car and entered a clean, small, garden apartment living room. While Lucy was in the kitchen preparing the cheesecake, my eyes fell upon an old-fashioned china closet full of porcelain figurines, and one especially stole my attention; a light gray Rosenthal Diana with the finest features I ever saw; a real museum piece.

"This is most beautiful," I said.

"One of my most precious possessions," Lucy exclaimed, as she gave me a delicious slice of cheesecake.

THE CATALYST

Several sessions later, Lucy called me to say a baby boy had been born in Detroit and she could get the baby.

"Lucy, it's a boy, and you have a name for a girl already picked out. Wait."

Lucy's choice was, "Susan Tov," and I felt she might raise a boy as a daughter; and then what?

The year was quickly coming to an end, and what about my promise to Lucy? As luck would have it, Lucy called me one Thursday to tell me that a child was going to be born next morning in Miami, Florida, and that she could have the child. The fee to a lawyer to make the birth certificate legal would be $1,000, and the airfare was $500. One difficulty was raising the money, as she did not have the cash and that was necessary.

"Send your parents to my office in New York City, and I'll loan you the $1,500, and as the baby will be born December 20, you'll return $100 per month on the 20th of each month until the $1,500 will be repaid."

On December 20, Susan Tov was born and I was declared her godfather. My promise came through, and Lucy became the mother of her daughter, just as she had planned for decades.

But the story doesn't end here. With the birth of Susan Tov, Lucy's depression lifted and her therapy ceased; she was not cured but her obsession disappeared. Each month, on the 21st or 22nd, I would receive a check for $100, made out on the 20th of the month. Lucy and Ken kept their word, just as I had during the August of the past year! After some six months, I had the privilege of meeting my godchild face to face, and this was a momentous occasion for me. I do not know how she took it. Time will tell. What I do know is that Lucy will make a distinguished mother, very loving, protective, and caring.

Many months later, all fifteen payments were made, and I was pleased to know that I made a significant difference to Lucy's depression, however obliquely, through Susan Tov's intervention. A few months later, a messenger delivered a large, imposing, square package which I proceeded to unwrap. After getting all the wrapping off, there was the beautiful Rosenthal Diana porcelain figurine with the following handwritten note:

"Dear Doc. Words cannot thank you enough for all that you have done for me and my family. I never forgot your expression when first you saw this figurine, and since it is my most prized possession, the one thing that if I give up I will miss forever, I want you to have it, forever. We all love you. Lucy."

MIND OVER MATTRESS

David was a thirty-two-year-old bachelor. However, one could hardly call him a bachelor in the truest sense of the word, as he was so immature, self-absorbed, and neurotic that he could be considered thirty-two going on seventeen.

He was an intelligent college graduate from a prestigious New England coed university. David never got over his mother's early demise when she was forty-eight and he was fourteen. The only child, he was raised by a tender, loving, understanding, generous father who was very devoted to his son. In college, David was introverted, bookish, and a social isolate, but got along with most of his roommates and students. In his sophomore year, he met a "sweet, introverted, neurotic Jewess."

From the beginning, they became a couple and were seen on the campus together almost always. They had meals together, worked in the library, studied, and went to extracurricular events, always together. After some months, they began sleeping together; that is, they became intimate sexually. As lovers, each was the first experience. David was pleased with himself, but not so with Jean. He knew from the start of their romance that this could not go anywhere. Jean, on the other hand, felt certain that she and David would someday be married. She promised him unconditional love, devotion, and exclusivity. He couldn't make any kind of commitment, and certainly not exclusivity. David found sex, as he referred to it, a matter of fact, not a matter of desire. Jean "was in heaven, each and every time we were intimate." This pretty much summed up their relationship for three years.

After graduation, the usual promises were made about keeping in touch, but David knew in his heart of hearts he would never see Jean again. She, however, kept hoping against hope.

David referred to his college romance as though it was the romance of the century, now that it was over. He obsessed in his ruminations about how great Jean was in bed, even though in therapy he remembered "it was a bore and I felt I was merely servicing her."

After Jean, there were several brief encounters at the usual singles' scenes, but there was more inspiration than perspiration. David began to obsess about sex and the process of sexual encounters with little actual activity. He was developing much angst and anxiety with tension headaches and heart palpitations. He was "striking out" at dances and singles weekends, and he "yearned for the good old days with Jean."

THE CATALYST

David had been an English major in college and took a masters degree in Journalism. He obtained a job at a small newspaper in a North Carolina college town. While there, he made the acquaintance of a young lady from the east who was a secretary in town. She was very attractive and sweet but not of the Jewish faith, and so he knew, right then and there, that this relationship would be limited. It, too, went on for three years, and Joanne fell madly in love with him. Asked if he loved her, he replied: "Not really, sex was not so good. Besides, she wasn't Jewish and she wanted to get married and have a child."

The tension between Joanne and David was getting unbearable, with her demanding that they get engaged or terminate this affair. This was really what David wanted to hear at that time, and so, it ended.

He returned to New York, where he got a job in the public relations department of a public utility corporation, which he despises. She met a young man on the rebound, got married, and today has a lovely son. On the rare occasions when he phones her, she tells David she still loves him. It must be his sense of humor, certainly not his sense of timing.

So much of David's sex life is fantasy and obsession that after each encounter, whether he tries for a one-night-stand or it lasts one or two weeks or three years, he adds more rumination and wishful thinking. Thus, he has a rich sex life in his mind with little acting out. While he attends dances and sees young women he would like to meet, by the time he makes his move, some other man is dancing with her or she has left with someone else. Weeks later, he may see the same woman, but this time she's not that attractive. Her legs have to be straight and long, her breasts large, her waist narrow, her face attractive.

Out of sheer desperation, he has dated quantity not quality, of late. He claims he is still selecting and not settling where women are concerned. Nonetheless, he betrays a demeanor of lust and longing rather than one of relaxed contemplation of "what will happen will happen." It must have been during one of these somber and thoughtful moods that David decided to return to therapy.

David immediately plunged into the topic closest to his mind and heart: sex. He began to relate several brief encounters he recently had with women whom he found inferior in one form or another. It was always easy for him to find fault with her. Usually, they looked fine at the dance, but during lunch or dinner of the first date he saw them close up and they were not as attractive as they had been that night or they looked better in jeans. Sometimes he found fault with their use of the English language or they were not really all that bright, etc., etc.

He related his last encounter with a forty-two-year-old, divorced saleslady and would-be singer.

"She was lying next to me and starts fumbling for my penis. I find it annoying...here is this lady ten to fifteen minutes afterwards and I'm not responding. So I brush her head away and I put my hands in that area. I don't think she 'came' because she did get out of bed. I asked her if she wanted to sleep. 'Not that tired, she said.' It used to bother and worry me a lot when I 'came' and the girl didn't. I used to try to have her come, somehow. But now, I'm so tired and out of it, spiritually exhausted and depressed; no motivation to deal with it.

"Throughout the night she stayed real close to me. I only had one small corner of the bed. She's a sweet person, dependent, and nice. I like her, but because of a combination of things, I'm not sexually excited. I don't want to deal with sex, it's too much trouble; more than it's worth. Even when I do have sex once, I want to be left alone. In the morning, I couldn't wait to get home to clean my house. Drove her home; only thing annoying about her is her New York accent. I guess the whole point about this story is I think I really didn't want to have sex with her at all. Too physically tired. Maybe if I really touched her and fooled around a lot I could have made an effort to 'come.'

"I knew only one woman who got my penis real hard. North Carolina in 1983. Not many women will do that for me. We met in a bar. She worked for a local weekly. I asked her if she wanted to come up to my apartment to see my terminal (computer, that is). When I went to the bathroom and returned she had taken off all her clothes. I was interested. It was momentous. I'm obsessed with my penis, but this was natural and I 'came' fast. An hour later, she touched me, I got hard and I 'came.' I guess she 'came' too. It happened again in the morning. I never had so much sex in such a short time.

"Now, I'm concerned sex isn't so great, maybe the first time is okay. During the day, I feel anguish about my virility. I have this energy in my body, but not in my penis or balls. Energy blocked. I have constant inferiority about this area, down below, my balls are small. They used to be bigger. I can feel no sexual desire when I sense they're smaller. When they get bigger I get desire.

"Last two nights I masturbated before sleeping and I felt better; energy dissipated. Eight years ago, it was more natural; now sex is hard work. Women and bodies used to be more exciting. Over the last four to five years, I could count the number of times I've had sex with different women. When I walk around every day I feel no desire, no effusive interest. I experience only feelings of inferiority, lack of confidence. No feelings in my balls or penis. I have masochistic thoughts; not that I would do anything. But I can visualize knives and things tearing me. It's not a big deal, these images, but sometimes they satisfy me. It's this sexual thing, the lack of excitement in my life.

THE CATALYST

"I was watching cable television and an ad for tonic for men with lack of desire. I thought, maybe I'm like these people. That disturbs me. Maybe first it's biological, but through lack of use it becomes psychosexual. I don't feel in my penis and balls like I used to. There are varying degrees of erection. My balls don't get big and full like they used to. I feel that they do get big when I have sex. I can sense and feel it. But I'm more concerned about lack of interest in sex even when I'm with someone."

"How often have you heard me say, 'You should have a relationship first and then sexual intimacy will come along with it?'"

He argued: "Concentrate on a relationship first? How will that help my reduced sexual desire?"

"You want to focus on sexual desire...I suggest you focus on your interest or lack of it in a relationship...the sex act will come later. A woman wants to be romanced and feel she is meaningful to a man, and after a period of dating time, when the setting is right, sexual intimacy can flourish. Some even require a commitment."

David persisted, "Why can't I be like I was eight years ago when I enjoyed sex?"

I countered, "You're different now; you've been through 'hard knocks' sexually."

Still he did not get the point. "I don't measure myself, but I know I'm smaller."

At the beginning of the next session I thought it propitious to discuss the concept of tumescence and detumescence, wherein the former is a state of swelling caused by a deposit of semen in the testicles, while the latter is a subsidence of erectile tissue of genital organs (penis and clitoris) following erection. However, in neither case can the person feel the swelling nor the subsidence in the penis nor in the clitoris. David listened to this explanation as though we were having a duologue rather than a dialogue; that is, he was not listening to me as much as preparing a rebuttal to counter my statements.

David began to pick up where we left off. "You ended by saying that I should get into a relationship. I agree that a relationship should come first and that I should take sex slowly and naturally. I'm not used to that. Over the months, since we've been talking, I've speculated on a few theories. Maybe I need some sex therapy to find out if it is physical, biological or hormonal? I don't feel good these days. I used to get excited, get hard, and then have sex. My potency isn't what it used to be."

"Why don't you explore some of the causes?" I suggested.

"About five years ago, I had more libido, more drive, more excitement."

"And you performed with distinction and satisfaction?" I interrupted.

"Well, sort of normal; I was satisfied more than I am now."

THE CATALYST

"And did you have intercourse two or three times a night in those golden days of your youth?"

"Well, no. It was like this. I'd go into a bar, meet a woman I was attracted to, and go back to her apartment. I'd talk to her, then screw her. We'd go to sleep. Next morning I'd screw again. I didn't worry then, I knew I could do it when I was in that kind of situation."

"So, now you have less confidence and are less satisfied with your performance?"

"Then, I was happier, more satisfied with my life in general. Now, I can't get hard in the morning. I think my lack of confidence is a factor. Perhaps, also, is the way I used to treat women. I must have given them a raw deal, just using them, I guess. Maybe it's true what my mother used to say: 'You get more love with honey than with vinegar.'"

"Five years ago, you were happier in North Carolina area than you are in the New York area. Also, you were a journalist then and now you feel you write like a hack."

"I don't even write at all, now."

"There are many reasons for your general malaise with yourself, and this is transported into the bedroom."

"I'm also concerned that the lack of use and infrequency will cause chronic atrophy of my entire psychosexual system."

"At age thirty-two, you feel your system is atrophied; I would hypothesize that it is more in your psychological responses than physiological in nature. Your problems are not in your hormones or anatomy, certainly not in atrophy of your system. If anything, it is hypertrophy of your ego, libido, and drive. You're saying that the circumference of your testicles is smaller now than it was in the past. You can feel that? You can see that?"

"Yes, why not! I look in the mirror and I can tell. They are! Who the hell doesn't look at their bodies? Now, the testicle is the size of a chick pea or the size of a pecan nut. The skin around it is there, but the actual size is smaller. I feel the emptiness!"

"You can feel the depletion in your testicles?"

"Yes, especially after I masturbate. I have to masturbate even to get it hard nowadays."

"In other words, you have to crank it up?"

"Yes! This weekend, I'm meeting Susan and driving out to the beach house on Friday night. She wants to do something Saturday and Sunday, but I don't want to."

"You know now that all you want to give her is twelve hours."

"Well, maybe a part of Saturday; provided she does not want intercourse on Saturday. If I don't feel like it, then I won't have sex, and if she does, the hell with her! Well, yes; I won't get hard anyway. It has happened 100 times before."

"You know now that you won't respond; it has happened in the past because you didn't want anything to happen. In Psychology 101, didn't you learn about the negative, self-fulfilling prophecy? Furthermore, in the same class didn't you learn about the positive self-fulfilling prophecy? David, you can *sexceed* if you set your mind to it; if you adopt a positive mental set!"

"Oh, I don't know, you're reading into my unconscious. Anyway, I don't have a lot of energy in the morning. I don't want to shock my system with sex." At this point, David laughs when he realizes the sophomoric argument he just posited.

I just could not allow David to espouse so many myths as he enunciated above, and I felt that I could appeal to his sense of fair play and empathy and the recent changes in feminism. I recommended he read Fromm's *The Art of Loving* and Gibran's *The Prophet* for starters, and the he try to alter his perceptions, or rather misconceptions, of women in general, and those he will date, specifically, in the future. He left rather bemused, but I felt encouraged.

David came for his next session and brought his copy of *The Art of Loving*. He claimed to have read this little tome in its entirety and found much of it helpful. He spoke of new relationships he had made with women and did not get involved sexually because he felt "the young women were not ready."

One morning, on his commuter bus coming in from New Jersey, David sat down alongside an attractive young woman. She noticed the book he was reading; namely, *The Art of Loving*. They began a conversation in which she admitted having read the book herself. Sharon was impressed with David's interest in such a book, and the discussion "was warm and friendly" David reported to me. The two began to date, and much of David's therapy concerned his affection for Sharon.

After two months of dating, David finally decided that they should go to Washington, D.C. for a long sightseeing weekend. Up until this time, there had been no sexual intimacy, but just the usual heavy petting and kissing. When I asked David why no sexual activity had occurred, he merely replied, "She's a nice person and I want to build toward something."

Sharon professed to be very fond of David and told him she was falling in love with him, whereupon he, too, felt that way about her. David's entire approach toward Sharon was different. The issue of sex did not even occur to him, but rather, the issue of a relationship, first.

During their weekend together, they experienced their first sex act, and David could not wait to tell me upon his return, "How great she was and how different intimacy is when you know the art of loving!"

JACK IS BACK

But Jack was really never away.

Jack was referred by another patient when both were students at Columbia University and both received masters degrees in Business Administration. Jack came to my office May 9, 1958, when he was twenty-seven years old, thin but balding. He was the eldest of three sons born to poor immigrant parents from Turkey. His father ran a mom-and-pop fruit and vegetable store in the South Bronx, and both parents insisted that their sons play musical instruments and acquire an education.

Jack had an Italian name, was a Sephardic Jew, and could talk fluent Spanish; all this came in handy in his decision to manage musicians and be an agent and booker in the music business. He also played many wind instruments and supervised his younger brother's musical career to the point where the latter was one of the country's youngest tympanists of a major symphonic orchestra. Thanks to Jack's supervision and filial devotion, his middle brother obtained a Ph.D. in Sociology; both brothers went on to raise ideal families of their own.

Jack is divorced and is racked with pain that he cannot afford to travel to a neighboring midwestern city to visit his sixteen-year-old son and thirteen-year-old daughter, who are living with their mother and supported by their millionaire, philanthropic grandfather. The injustices are many and the self-recriminations plentiful, to the point where self-hate and aggression coalesce into a syndrome of clinical depression.

When he was asked what was the greatest lack in his childhood, he replied, "It's not fair for me to say love and understanding. But possibly, more intelligent or capable parents—I don't mean as parents or people. But I feel that I needed someone to help me get a clearer and sounder understanding of life to get me started at that time. This is just a feeling but I'm not too sure as to whether I'm justified in even this feeling."

At twenty-seven Jack was still searching for succor himself, but found none at home. Indeed, it was he who had to play the role of father to both of his brothers. He insisted that the youngest practice, practice, practice; hours at a time was not enough. It was Jack who cajoled and often hit his brother, which the latter has never forgotten, despite his successes; except now, he, too, wonders whether music was his real calling. As for the middle brother, Jack had to make a quick trip to Italy to gather him up after a torrid love affair in which the latter was about to enter into a senseless marriage.

THE CATALYST

Jack always behaved as a dutiful son and brother. No one held out a helping hand when he needed one. Thus, he was resentful, angry, anxious, lonely, and full of remorse and aggression. He was just as needy and unfulfilled when it came to women, also. He often took up with the secretaries and girl fridays, as they were called in those pre-feminist days. After a while, he would be abusive and expect more and more and more.

As a matter of fact, sooner or later, his demands of his help, male as well as female, became inordinate. Frequently, arguments developed, and they would leave after much hard feelings, and he would often feel betrayed. He developed suspicious tendencies, almost bordering on the paranoid, accusing his employees of stealing clients and lists.

During these halcyon days, Jack was successful, with more gigs than he could control; yet he tried to be on top of all situations simultaneously. During one weekend, he might have three weddings, two bar mitzvahs, two corporate functions, and two vocalists he managed. He would attend all dates to make certain nothing went wrong; something frequently did. He would call me two or three times a day before signing contracts, and three or four times a day after the signing; he would call me about how to manage his staff and how to respond to a prospective client. Frequently, after hanging up, he would call again immediately with a new thought he had about an issue.

Jack was addicted to the phone. The phone became his lifeline and the umbilical cord to his society. Not only did he run up exorbitant bills, but he made a first-class nuisance of himself with staff, prospective clients, former clients, family, and me, in particular. However, I never remember hanging up on him; perhaps I should have!

No matter how busy he was, and he always appeared busy, talking to several people on the phone almost simultaneously all over the country and often overseas, he always had something in his mouth; solid foods or liquids. Jack had an addictive personality; addictive to talk, the telephone, and food. His addictive personality was to be his undoing. He was obsessed with the music business, and because he gave it almost eighteen hours a day, he expected the same devotion from his staff, which he never got. Because he usually flew off in ten different directions, he often gave the impression of being disorganized, which he was and so was his office and so was his personal life.

Jack was not a Johnny-come-lately; Jack was a Jack-come-lately. He had an undiagnosed reading disability in school which left him with a poor .self-concept and a marked sense of inferiority and lack of confidence. In this thirties, he put on massive amounts of weight and had trouble taking pounds off; he grew a beard and resembled a benign Santa Claus. Almost pushing forty, Jack met a young lady from Ohio and he began a whirlwind romance in person, but mostly by phone. During this time, he consulted me regularly several times a week, but also had me on the phone twenty or thirty times per week. By now, Jack had become quite dependent on me for matters concerning his business, his family, and his personal life; I was a font of information; all information. Apparently, I knew everything about everything!

What I didn't know was the fact that Jack and his bride were abusing pot. "in this business everyone uses a little 'pot,' Doc." Business was still booming, and June, his wife, fitted in beautifully until their son was born and June became a full-time mother. From what I heard and observed, June never became a full-time wife because, even before her son appeared, she was a full-time daughter of her father's. Jack's complaint was correct; June never committed to the marriage.

Not getting the recognition, attention, and affection at home, Jack sought this at work and kept unusually long hours at his business. By this time, he had learned how to become a hustler and, while devoted to his son, he was not overjoyed when his daughter was born four years later. Even during this time of seeming success, financial help from his father-in-law was necessary for personal expenses and loans for his business.

Jack was so disorganized that he could not tell anyone, his wife, his accountant, his father-in-law, nor his banker what his profit-and-loss sheet would look like. He did not know how much he earned in any one month or how much business he did and how much he owed and how much was owed to him. This drove his father-in-law, a very successful businessman, literally to distraction, and he was loathe to lend Jack further monies to fill a bottomless pit.

In his fifties, Jack spoke to me as often as usual, but was seeing me less and less and, apparently, June had found a "therapist" her neighbor "used" and so she and Jack both "consulted" him. I use the quotation marks, as this individual was not credentialed nor certified and, indeed, was abusing cocaine with both of them. To be sure, Jack and June were "turning on" regularly, and Jack learned how to "free-base" like an expert and was "into the very best available."

This was the beginning of the end. I was no longer in the picture. Jack was going from bad to worse, neglecting even his first love, his music business. At the late age of fifty-two, Jack had become an addict but would not or could not admit it. If he had, his wife could have prevailed upon her father to pay for his hospitalization. In any event, his family might have rallied around him and given him the supports so necessary in drug addiction rehabilitation. As it was, none of his brothers understood his illness, and his wife left him with their two children and returned to her family. June sued for divorce and got everything. Jack lost his business, his office, his phone ad listing in the yellow pages, his home, and his children—everything. He was devastated and still is!

THE CATALYST

In the last few years, Jack is back; back with me, that is. Fortunately, he discovered AA and CA and attends meetings with regularity, sometimes two or three a day and night. He leads, he qualifies, he sponsors, he literally does everything he is supposed to do, and then some. Without these group experiences, he would not have survived, and today he is healthier emotionally than he ever was in his sixty years. He has gained insight but is still in great pain.

He moved into his mother's old rent-controlled apartment in the northern part of the Bronx, and each Sunday at 8:45 A.M. I meet his express bus and we drive to breakfast and his session with me. He tells me how much he is indebted to me for sticking by him. He jogs regularly, takes Lithium in a small dose, and is disciplined by keeping the early Sunday morning session with me. After breakfast, he starts his rounds of three or four meetings toward sobriety. He is looking forward to his third anniversary of "being clean."

He still calls me at least once or twice a day, and is searching for advice or just succor or just to see if I'm still there. Throughout our relationship, I have helped with loans to pay rent, for food, for his phone bills; never for drugs. I have done more than "just listen," I have been there and I have understood, just as his sixteen-year-old son has understood, as revealed by the following poem he sent Jack. I reproduce it with both of their permission because I feel it could help others come back.

FOR MY FATHER

It was your mistake
But not your fault
For, you, like the mouse,
Went after the cheese.

They were poison berries.
You knew not of their venom.
Like an abandoned bridge,
You knew not its capacity.

But nobody is perfect.
Nobody should be,
For if you were,
Why bother waking up?

The more stones you trip over
The better you become
At getting back up,
So walk with confidence.

THE CATALYST

For now you know
What berries to pick,
What bridges to cross.
Now you know.

So walk with agility
Through the forest.
Run when you like.
Sit when you're tired.

But always know,
No matter how big I get,
I'll always feel the joy
Of riding on your shoulders.

So let's start over from here.
Get down on your knees
So I can climb up,
And we'll travel together,
Father and son.

There are universes to cover,
But you need not hurry.
We'll savor each step
And enjoy each moment.

But before we start,
I want you to know
That I have confidence in you
Regardless of mile markers.

Jeremy Jason Adato

THE NOBLE PHILOSOPHICAL HAND

When he was sixteen, Arthur was brought to my office for intellectual and aptitudinal assessment. He was administered a complete psychodiagnostic battery with psychoeducational and projective techniques. On the Wechsler Adult Intelligence Scales, he achieved verbal IQ of 141, very superior; performance IQ of 93, low average; full-scale IQ of 121, superior intelligence; but the spread in verbal and performance IQs suggest social isolation, introversion, social awkwardness, and poor learning skills. As a matter of fact, the major reason for his mother bringing him for assessment was the fact that he wanted to "drop out of high school and stay home and educate himself." His mother also reported that he was very suspicious, belligerent, anxious, and "talking out of his head."

He was almost paranoid about his sessions with me, wondering who would know about what he says in my office, the FBI, CIA? His speech was rambling, with flights of ideas and thoughts running into each other with no apparent relationship. He was very verbal, but not oriented for time, place, and events. Contained in his speeches was evidence that he was very well-read and that he had accumulated a great deal of irrelevant knowledge and information, particularly in the areas of literature, philosophy, and politics. He read constantly when at home, and would often stay awake all thought the night and fall asleep in the morning, thereby not going to school. Despite these unusual habits and talking in a rambling fashion at home and school, he was earning an 86 high school average and would graduate with his class. His mother and teachers definitely felt Arthur was "sick."

He was unable to sit still and would get up and walk about the room and talk in a rambling, circuitous fashion. Much of his verbiage contained neologisms, peppered with psychoanalytic jargon, and political and media terminology. None of it ever made much sense, but I listened intently and gave him my most serious attention. He invariably wanted esoteric, psychoanalytical explanations such as penis envy, castration complex, and incest wish for almost all behavioral manifestations. Frequently, all explanations were irrelevant, as he rambled on and paid no heed to me except to cast me in a suspicious light. Despite his seeming annoyance with me, Arthur kept his appointments for "philosophical relief" as he referred to them. However, he resented any interruptions: "I like people to listen to me since I have a lot of ideas and I need to talk about them."

Despite bizarre and illogical outbursts in school, he was graduated and accepted to Park College, a small liberal arts college near Kansas City, Missouri. He lasted six months and had to be picked up by his mother, as the school authorities could not handle him or his psychosis, as their psychiatrist put it. He spoke of his birth in Miami Beach, Florida, and growing up in Brooklyn, New York, but was out of place in the heartland of American discussing Freud, Kant, Spinoza, Einstein, JFK, FDR, and Eisenhower, just for starters. He was misunderstood, ridiculed, and abused, mostly by fellow students who did not have the vaguest notion of what he was talking about. All of this tumult played into his paranoid machinations, and he and mother were finally able to accept my reticence for recommending Park College in the first place. Just another failure that Arthur had to deal with.

When he returned to Brooklyn, he started to see me again and went to a psychiatrist for medications which he took with regularity. The latter kept the schizophrenic process in check, so for years, his illness was contained. He would make grandiose plans for his future careers, which were unrealistic. He lacked insight, not only into the nature of his illness, but also about the poor prognosis paranoid schizophrenia augured. In therapy with me, he frequently referred to the psychological tests he had taken years before and he looked forward to additional ones "in order to prove his abilities over the years."

His sessions were reduced to once a week, and we discussed many topics about current events and life situations at home with his mother and stepfather, with whom he got on exceedingly well.

Every now and then, he demanded psychoanalytic explanations for thoughts he entertained that did not require such explanations in the first place. Arthur saw everything in terms of castration anxiety, penis envy, transference, id, and superego. It was as though he had read one of Freud's books and this altered the direction of his entire life. Another authority that he quoted over and over again and again was Dale Carnegie, of *How To Win Friends And Influence People* fame. Unfortunately, he did not have the emotional stability to digest and understand most of the authors he read at the height of his mental illness.

After one of our sessions, I received a phone call from the local police precinct that Arthur had accosted an officer on the street in one of his paranoid episodes and had been taken to Bellevue Psychiatric Hospital. His mother had him stay there for thirty days, and then he was transferred to a private psychiatric hospital. He was given about fifty electric shock treatments, and then sent to Pilgrim State Hospital on Long Island, where he stayed for almost ten years. Arthur went from bad to worse, and fixated his illness on two psychiatrists. Fortunately, paranoid schizophrenic patients do not deteriorate as much as other types of schizophrenic patients, so that when he was discharged during the deinstitutionalized movement of sending patients out into the community mental health centers, Arthur or his mother or both remembered his sessions with me, and so he returned, older, fatter, grayer, and sicker.

He was very flattering to me and great for my ego, as he found me to be much more intelligent than I was. He also always made reference, much to my embarrassment, to how well-groomed I was. In addition, he began to refer to "my noble philosophical hands" which revealed, to him, my longevity and considerable erudition. He also apologized for having "chosen the two psychiatrists in the State Hospital" over me and talked about Drs. Hermann and Brock constantly. The community health centers never eventuated, but Arthur received medication from a local hospital as an outpatient and came to me frequently, one or twice a week, for psychotherapy. During these sessions, we discussed additional tests he took periodically, dreams, relationships with his stepfather and mother, his plans for realistic career goals, and my "noble philosophical hands." During the past decade of the '80s he did not get into any difficulty with the police or the law, nor did he require any further hospitalization. Throughout these many decades, he has been one of my "reduced fee" patients, which he never fails to acknowledge by reaffirming, "I appreciate your generosity for seeing me, and God bless."

As evidence of schizophrenic ideation and how our sessions progress, we offer the following unabridged dialog.

"You know what I once did? Some man was begging for money with a paper coffee cup. I put some money in and said, 'Bonjour Valjean.' Isn't that funny? I thought one of my teeth was getting an abscess, but the swelling went down. I thought I would have to go to the dentist and couldn't keep my appointment. I wanted to come to see you. I have holes on the outside of my teeth. I lived in a mythological world and I was very intelligent, my test scores proved it. I feel, after reading Plato, that there is a higher power, but it has mathematical limitations. You are a great genius, a better genius than me. Time Magazine had an article about 500 psychiatrists and asked them if the cold war was coming back. Also, an article about Coca Cola and diseases you can catch from drinking it. People think Mozart was a good pianist but his wife was always nagging him. He'd run into the living room and play instead of having sex (laughs for twenty seconds). What do you think? Did Washington have a large penis? People think he did. He was Aquarius. If you have a small penis how do you overcome the handicap?

THE CATALYST

"They call him the American man, but they don't know what American is. Women want to be noble. Are the men noble while they're doing it to a Jewish woman? Is a man more noble than a Jewish woman? It might change in a generation. What do you think of New York, of the Waldorf-Astoria? Of the people who made sacrifices, a powerful image, especially of the Russians. My uncle once told me, the only thing Israel wants is a masterful race, like Russia. You have 'noble and philosophical hands.' Women love it. Christ was talking with one noble philosophical hand. I always wanted a relationship with a woman, but I don't have the hands. Do you think that you could make me so intellectual that I could hold my own at Columbia? Say in about two years. I'm starting to read Aristotle's 'Logic.' I'm getting confused but it is a good idea. That's a computer so you can 'logic-tate.' If X is a noun and Y is an adjective and the difference between X=black and Y=white and if X square = X and Y square = Y and XX-0 and YY=0 there are only two sets and what's the difference between black and white? Really I have a mathematical intellect and an intellectual mind. I read the 'History of Intellectuals' going back to the Greeks saying that in mathematical and intellectual times good was transformed into the good and the good into time and then the mathematical goes on to transform it into the good and intellectual. And then X=X, then X=sex, then X=0, 1=0, X square=X, then X=sex=0. Then everything=everything because X=X. Then we have to be mathematical, because as long as things are mathematical it is just the same in life.

"What do you think of the cold war? It occurred to me that I could go to Chicago for $100 without being caught. I'd walk down to the plane and toward the baggage. 'Sir, can I count the luggage?' And he doesn't check the number of the airplane I'm going on. And it's the same airplane that I'm coming back on over the weekend. It's the same $100. I once went to Kansas City and met two girls from the Bronx. Would make a good title for a book or a song (laughs for twenty-five seconds)."

On other occasions Arthur asked me, "When a woman castrates a man symbolically what does that mean?"

"What do you think?"

"A woman fears not being loved; a fear of rejection."

"You're very good and intelligent. You remind me of Einstein. I see you more than just a psychologist. I see you as having attended Harvard Law School, and now being Dean of NYU or Harvard Law School.

"I'd like to get my hands on the Yellow Pages and look up local astrologers. I used to have the Yellow Pages but lost it. I want to find out when I should be baptized. I want to join the Salvation Army, which is a subdivision of the Church. I want to give my life to Christ and join the Salvation Army. I want to go back to high school and get an honors diploma and go to college to become a psychologist or a social worker and supervise social workers in the Salvation Army as a psychologist. My character would be strengthened. I wouldn't be a phony or a common gangster. I want to be sincere in my calling.

"The true Evangelists of Christianity on Kings Highway on Avenue J in Brooklyn is called The Labor Center. 'You are going to be an Evangelist before you die,' said the priests there. St. Paul and St. Peter were both reincarnated as Asher, the tribe of Israel.

"Your mustache and hair look very good. Did you cut your hair and mustache? And your level of concentration is very elegant. You're getting to be the way you were before. You're charismatic, like my heavenly father. With your promise you should have gone to Harvard. You are a gentle person. Can you help me come out of this? I'm almost completely recovered, but I still need to be told what the past M.D.s did and why they did it, and why I love this nervousness. I think it was oral austerity and incestuous conflict. That's my opinion.

"Could be separation anxiety or some neurophysiological chemical imbalance or is it hysteria. I may have reached the heart of the incest solution and I have not reached my potential. You keep saying I'm very intelligent but I will not attend Harvard and I must have some other handicaps. Could it be that I have been taking medication for more than thirty years that kept me from reaching my potentials? Or did my father's penis have hysterical symptoms? I don't understand why you won't tell me the Freudian reasons concerning my case. Why don't you tell me, Dr. Weider?"

"I don't think your illness need be explained by Freudian reasons; theorists of your illness offer biochemical explanations."

"That's not true. The body controls the biochemical. I read that ulcers come from emotions; high blood pressure comes from emotions. The biochemical also comes from personal emotions. They are so interlocked that one depends upon drugs. But I found that the biochemistry needs to be safe, for neurotic reasons, and there is a biochemical correspondence by emotional things. And I want to know about Freudian insights."

I asked, "Why did they give you drugs and electric shock at all the hospitals, private and public, that you were in?"

"Well, the drugs helped me forget so I wouldn't have to suffer nor remember what had happened and the same for electric shock treatments."

THE CATALYST

I continued, "You were unusually sensitive, introverted, and intelligent. You read everything you got your hands on and remembered most of it with excellent comprehension. In addition, you lacked friends and were considered odd and soon became isolated. Like Immanuel Kant, who at thirteen was alone, because no one could understand this little German boy, you, too, found no one who could understand you. In addition, either a gene or some biochemical imbalance or both could be reasons that you became ill more than thirty years ago."

After listening attentively, Arthur said: "Oh, I see." And immediately offered, "Well I had a word from Mars where I feel they had a cloak about me, and other people from Brooklyn and they heard about Socrates, and Aristotle had a lisp. And it is that type of intelligent person, like Sinclair Lewis and Marty that identify with writing about people on the street. And the liberals and Arthur Miller were saying the same thing. What did you think of JFK, Truman, and General MacArthur?

"I discovered something. St. Peter and St. Paul were both Ashers. Next time I come will you give me a battery of tests. You told me when I first came, more than thirty years ago, that you would. I don't want tests on mathematics, I want the full battery of tests that you once were going to give me. I want to test my competence. Will you do that for me?

"You look very good. You have personal powers in your appearance, and very charismatic. I got here a half hour early and I smoked a cigar by a car. Someone offered me marijuana for $20 and some for $5. I told him next time I see him I'll get some, but I don't want it now. I don't like traveling in the city with 'pot' on me. I don't want to take the risk. Would you have your patients smoke marijuana while they talked with you? It's a good idea, helps them to see things differently.

"Don't you find that all German doctors treat their patients good? God was telling them to treat them well. The German M.D.s aren't anti-semitic, the Jewish psychologists said, after the war was over. They just thought they were some kind of supermen. What do you think of Bob Dylan?"

"Why do you ask?"

"Just curious. I have some old tapes at home. I like the music but don't understand the poetry.

"I'm going to the library on Thursday and take out a copy of poetry by William Blake. If they don't have a copy I'll read the reference book all night Thursday. I'll finish it on Friday and Saturday. Then I'll read all the criticisms, and then maybe I'll understand poetry. Will you recommend a collection or volume of poets and their criticisms? I want to make a study of certain poets. Will you do that for me?"

I said, "Sure."

"I have to get some law books. I can't find any books by Jung. I once took out a book about the archetypes of the unconscious. I didn't read much, but I enjoyed what I read. Would you write a book about psychology for undergraduates? Books that could be understood. You are so charismatic and effective that I can see you writing for undergraduates like me. Books to treasure. Why don't you write philosophy?"

"I'm not a philosopher."

"I think you are. Every psychologist is a philosopher. It's part of his soul. That's why I want you to treat me."

I GOT IT

Marie was an undergraduate student in an evening course I taught at Hunter College in the fall of 1947. Toward the end of the semester, she approached my desk and announced that she would like to major in Psychology toward her goal of getting a Ph.D. "If you would like, why don't you discuss this further with me during my office hour?"

A few days later, we had a session in which she filled me in about her difficult economic and social situation. Marie and her three children were living on welfare in a one-bedroom flat in an old tenement building on the east side near Hunter; her alcoholic husband had deserted her and their children without any forewarning and funds years ago. She worked as a stenographer and secretary during the day and attended Hunter four evenings a week. She studied while her babies slept; their ages were three, five, and seven. Her neighbors volunteered as babysitters. Weekends were time out for children, shopping, cleaning, library research, and more studying. I had to admire this woman's determination, tenacity, persistence, and pure gumption.

I was hard-pressed to point out the many obstacles that lay before her in her quest to get a Ph.D. I must confess, I tried to dissuade her by being realistic in terms of sacrifices, financial and economic, emotional and social, and as a single parent raising three little ones. She would have none of it, but was as determined as ever to go forward with her plans to major in Psychology and get her bachelor's, master's, and eventually, I guess, her Ph.D. She earned an A in class.

Marie went her way, and I went to the University of Louisville School of Medicine in Louisville, Kentucky. During late August 1950, I was at the American Psychological Association convention held that year on the campus of the Pennsylvania State University. I had just arrived, settled into my dorm room, freshened up, and decided to walk across the campus to register, when I heard my name called several times. I turned around and, much to my surprise, was warmly greeted by Marie. Apparently, she had noticed my name in the program as one of the presenters of a paper and she knew, therefore, that I would be in attendance at these meetings and she could see me.

She filled me in about the last few years. Yes! She did get her bachelors and masters degrees and had hoped that through my good offices, contacts, and colleagues, perhaps I could now help her with a dissertation topic for research and, better still, help her gain admission to some university for the doctorate. Her children were fine, healthy, and doing well in school. She was still a single parent. We exchanged room and phone numbers. I told her that I would be seeing lots of friends and colleagues at these meetings, both in formal and informal settings, and that, as a matter of fact, I was invited to several cocktail parties given by publishers and universities. In any case, she would hear from me by tomorrow, to which she remarked that she would see me tomorrow when I delivered my paper. I knew I was assured of applause from at least one.

We parted, and once again, I had to admire this young woman's persistence and perseverance. I was pleased and impressed at her overcoming so many obstacles in her personal and economic deprivations and, against all odds, sticking to her plans. I thought that she deserved to be rewarded.

That very evening, I attended a cocktail party and was mingling with new and old friends and exchanging many pleasantries when I was greeted by a colleague from Vanderbilt University who held similar posts as I at their medical school. In the course of our discussion, he asked me a question that amazed me. He wondered whether I had any graduate students or knew of any who were mature and willing to relocate for their doctorate and to participate in a very interesting sociopathological experiment. Funding was obtained to house a group of delinquents that would be divided into a control and experimental group, each supervised by the graduate student; controls would be given minimum food, clothing, shelter, and schooling while the latter would be showered with TLC and rewards for learning. The effects on their delinquency behavior would be studied.

I told him of Marie and inquired whether her three children would be a complicating factor. He assured me they would not. I told him of her maturity and tenacity and he was impressed also. He agreed to come to my presentation tomorrow and we three would confer. That evening, I left a note in Marie's mailbox and told her of the possibility of studying at Vanderbilt University.

The following morning, I gave my paper to an unusually large audience for a nine o'clock presentation, and after the session ended, the three of us met. I merely introduced the two and took leave, but did tell Marie to keep me posted throughout the meetings. I would keep my antennas out for other opportunities.

Two days later, I was leaving a meeting of psychologists, all of whom had medical school appointments, when Marie found me once again. This time she had a grin on her face, from ear to ear, and related the good news that she had been selected for the job and with it she would obtain a full scholarship to the doctoral program at Vanderbilt, if she passed the qualifying exams. She would receive a furnished apartment in the house and get room and board for herself and her children. In addition, there were provisions for a small financial stipend. Furthermore, some part of this sociopathological research could be submitted for her own doctoral dissertation and published later. Marie thanked me profusely and we parted.

I returned to Louisville feeling just fine. My paper was well received, my good deed had been achieved, and I started work on my two volumes: *Contributions Toward Medical Psychology.* I was consumed with the latter and with supervising psychology interns and teaching medical students and psychiatric residents and examining clinical patients, and working on a few research ideas for publication.

Year later, I returned to Cornell University Medical College-New York Hospital. Research papers were published and the two volumes appeared, but one day I received a two-cent postcard from Murfreesboro, Tennessee, postmarked January 31, 1955, which gave me more of an adrenalin "rush." Its message, pure and simple: "I got it. Marie M., Ph.D."

DRUG USER
TO PHARMACIST
TO PHARMACOLOGIST
TO THERAPIST

May 15, 1971, when he was twenty-two, Edward appeared at my office looking for guidance and succor. He was scattered somewhere in the middle of six children, all separated by about a year and a half or two. All of these children were very bright, tenacious, argumentative, belligerent, suspicious, and terribly neurotic. They were all the product of a middle-class "battler" of a father who started his hard life on the streets of the lower East Side, where in order to survive in the '30s, one had to be facile with his fists. Ralph was, and soon was good enough to be an amateur boxer, taxi driver, salesman, and then U.S. Postal Service mail deliverer, and soon supervisor.

Unfortunately, Ralph had a major heart attack and had to go on disability for the next thirty-five years. He then pursued his real love and became an actor in movies and television, but never achieved stardom. But he ego was assuaged, and for him that was sufficient.

During this time, his wife was dutifully engaged as mother and nurse and arbiter to all arguments, verbal and physical, between Ralph and some of his sons. Discussions were numerous and loud and dangerous. This was a family with much acting out, debates, and overflow of emotions; all leading to physicality.

Edward was about to complete college with a major in Chemistry, and was unrealistically planning a medical school education abroad. Without funds and encouragement from home and with a meager grade point average, another course of action had to be found to fulfill his unconscious, and sometimes conscious, wish to become a doctor. Experimentation with marijuana was a necessity to survive in the streets of Queens and Brooklyn, where Edward lived with his family. "Just Say No" could not work in the '70s anymore than it worked in the '80s. Fortunately, experimentation ceased when we found a natural career choice; namely pharmacy. Edward enrolled in what was to be the last class at Columbia University School of Pharmacy, where he graduated Summa Cum Laude in 1975. He was now on his way to financial independence and on his way, it turned out, to a doctorate, after all.

Soon after, he won his license as a registered pharmacist and was able to earn sufficient funds to support himself and his brother, who roomed with him on the East Side of Manhattan. All during this time, Edward was in weekly therapeutic sessions with me on a reduced-fee basis, and we then decided to have him try for the Ph.D. in Pharmacology. He applied at the Downstate Medical Center in Brooklyn, was accepted, and after a long and arduous course of study and experimentation and dissertation writing, finally, in 1979, was awarded the doctorate he so longed for when first he consulted me way back in 1971.

During this period, Edward published three articles in major pharmacological journals, but was supporting himself as a pharmacist in and around New York City. We realized that if he wished to compete in the academic arena, he would have to win a postdoctoral fellowship. Edward reached for the stars and applied to various prestigious medical school departments of Pharmacology, and the Massachusetts Institute of Technology. He was accepted at MIT. Being accepted was a new experience for Edward; not that he wasn't accepted by academic institutions, but being accepted by colleagues was another issue altogether. He was perceived as arrogant and belligerent, but actually, he was creative and innovative, and professional jealousy could be more accurate in the atmosphere of pressure for government and foundation funding. The test of this thesis was the many publications, peer reviewed, that Edward produced, all testifying to first-rate research. He began to excel as a teacher, also, and was revered by his students in graduate programs and professional schools.

Frequently, Edward would come to New York City from Cambridge to see his family, and he would have several sessions with me. It soon became apparent that his three years at MIT had produced several significant publications and that it was time to move on. As academic or pharmaceutical jobs were not available in the New York area, he applied for and was hired as a research associate in the Department of Neurology at Cornell University Medical College, Burke Rehabilitation Center, White Plains.

Now that he was living in New Rochelle, he started therapy sessions once again and was able to deal with intrapsychic and interpersonal issues concerning self, family, women, and colleagues. The more time he was spending in the laboratory, the more he preferred teaching, writing, and editing. However, here, too, he published, and even went to Italy to deliver a well-received paper.

Life with various women was more tortuous than pleasurable, and finances were always a problem, interfering with a marriage commitment. He was an obsessive, possessive, and jealous lover, always giving more than any one woman was capable or willing to give in return. His need for love was limitless and he was a passionate romantic.

The saxophone also became his avocation, and he found time for lessons and practice. Whatever Edward discovered, he pursued with intensity and diligence. And whatever he pursued, he achieved to the point of satisfaction. He adored cats with the same affection he demonstrated toward his women. He was devoted, caring, tender, and protective. Also, as the years passed, he became closer to his siblings and parents and they all began to realize that he was special.

After leaving the laboratory, his scientific knowledge took him to editing pharmaceutical handbooks for medical and nursing professions while teaching either full-time or as an adjunct professor.

It was during the latter stage that he realized that a career as psychotherapist might be the most rewarding "calling" he would like to pursue. Consequently, he applied and was accepted for the doctorate in Psychology. His maturity, personal psychotherapy, training and experience in Pharmacology, and scientific attitude all contributed to his acceptance. He excelled, so much so that he was invited to teach at the institution he attends, and is doing an examplary job with clients in psychotherapy. Furthermore, he is at work on a handbook for psychologists who will soon have prescription-writing privileges. As a licensed registered pharmacist with a doctorate in Pharmacology and a doctorate in Psychology engaged in psychotherapy, few will be better qualified to write the definitive pharmacopoeia of drugs for psychologists and psychotherapists. Edward has come a long way.

CEREBRAL CASTRATION

Helen was a thirty-four-year-old female patient who was born in Indianapolis, Indiana. She had been divorced after four years of married life; there were no children. She served nine months as a WAC, but her illness was not service-connected; yet she received a small monthly pension from the government. She was evaluated quite extensively, both by the psychiatric staff and the psychological unit, prior to unilateral lobotomy which she referred to as "cerebral castration."

Helen had been a disturbed child in a household of seven siblings who were not cared for properly; they were dirty, unfed, and uncared for by an unstable, alcoholic father after their mother died when Helen was four years old. Helen had been hospitalized on eighteen different occasions and had spent about 856 days in mental institutions; the overall length of her hospitalizations for mental conditions was a span of fourteen years. Her longest period of "normalcy" was a seven-year period from October 1936 to October 1943, during which she was married for four years.

Helen had been diagnosed as a manic depressive (manic) seven times and manic depressive (depressive) two times. She was diagnosed as a mixed manic depressive three times. She was also diagnosed as having mixed psychosis four times, unknown psychosis two times, and homosexuality four times. To further complicate the psychiatric picture, she was given at least fifty-one electric shock treatments; possibly as many as 100. The patient had been prescribed the usual medications, but was not cooperating in taking them on her own. She reluctantly agreed to the lobotomy.

Helen's mental illness, before the unilateral prefrontal labotomy ran the typical manic course. Just prior to her last hospitalization, she wrote, "and my boyfriend! I hope I never have to replace him. I could not do it. I mother him and, best of all, he mothers me. I am the happiest woman alive. I have moved to Palo Alto and have the most beautiful and spacious and cheapest apartment in California. We're living in sin and love it; we both know that love isn't free, but the price is nominal."

Sometime after this, the patient's manic stage took a swing up and she became very high, very free, and very gay, and in another subsequent letter, she wrote: "When I first came to California, I was another Don Quixote with a sweater that had a coat of arms and a hat like a helmet. I righted wrong in cheap bars and gave money to hungry sailors. Soon I grew tired of this and sealed my fate by undressing in an art gallery on the campus of Stanford University. There was no one around and there was a statue which reminded me of Narcissus. I kissed it. About that time the police came; I went to jail, was judged insane, and was admitted to the Palo Alto State Hospital with a room across the hall from my brother."

Helen claims that she has never really loved anyone other than her husband, although she has had numerous boyfriends and has, at times, been known to boast about her ability to "have any man I want, married or single." She is hesitant to discuss her married life and, especially, the cause of her divorce. Following her divorce, her manic phase had very definite cycles. Her sister is the only member of her family who is making a successful adjustment; indeed she is a leading figure in local society. Her sister claims the marriage was one of two emotionally immature persons thrown together with no courtship and quickly married after two weeks. Soon the newlyweds faced reality and found, much to their joint amazement, that two cannot live as cheaply as one. After many financial difficulties and more quarrels, they decided that divorce was the solution. He was a reporter who also drank and had been diagnosed as an alcoholic.

As for her sexual history, Helen was first exposed to homosexuality at the early age of four in a local institution for delinquent and dependent children, when an older girl slipped into bed with her and masturbated her. She forgot this instance until two years later when the same thing happened with a different girl. She had no definite crushes or attachments to advisors, teachers, or older females. In one of her hospitalizations, she showed an undue amount of interest in a sixteen-year-old manic, former girlfriend at the same institution. They were caught in bed caressing one another on several occasions.

As far as her heterosexual life was concerned, it started at sixteen, when she ran away to Chicago where she used a pseudonym and got mixed up with a gang of bootleggers. Among them was Charlie Capone. She also did striptease, acted as a gang moll, and slept with whomever would give her shelter for the night. This activity led to her first breakdown and hospitalization, which was in Chicago. Since then, her sex life has been one of overindulgence and promiscuity—she claims she does not want intercourse unless she gets drunk enough so that it does not matter, but that she does not get too drunk that she does not enjoy it. She said little about her present sexual activities, but one could gather that she was not abstaining, as her philosophy about any indulgence is: "I want what I want when I want it, and I usually get it in double helpings."

The patient's childhood was full of disappointments for herself and her seven brothers and sisters. Her mother died when she was four. Her father was diagnosed as a psychopathic personality who tried, but easily admitted defeat, in keeping the family together. Little Helen grew up at the institution referred to above for delinquent and dependent children, and has had one foster mother after another until finally she came to distrust everyone, saying, "No one understood me—no one tried."

An older brother had been a patient at the Palo Alto Veterans Administration Hospital for six years, suffering from dementia praecox or schizophrenia precipitated by World War II and, more especially, by the Italian campaign. This brother also had epileptic seizures and he was the one Helen met when she was hospitalized there.

Little was known about the adjustment of Helen's other siblings. In the sixteen years, from 1921 to 1937, she lived in twenty-two different places. All of this unrest and moving around caused the precipitation of her mental and emotional condition and led to her running away to Chicago and a long series of subsequent hospitalizations.

Helen's mental examination indicated an attitude and general behavior of definite mood swings from happy and cooperative one day, to arrogance and snappiness the next. At times, she let loose with a violent explosion of vulgar remarks, usually precipitated by the nurses' failure to have a cigarette ready for her at a specified time. She was no social mixer—always away from the rest of the patients. She frequently feigned being asleep to keep from listening to "some bitch's troubles." At times, she seemed calm and well-composed, and yet she had an impulse disorder which she could not control. Her speech was excellent, with good diction and care given to proper grammar. She deliberated when answering questions and would use, "I don't know," for questions she did not care to answer, so as not to divulge information she did not want the examiner to know.

Her stream of mentation was normal, except for explosive outbursts of vulgarity when she got upset, which was often and quite sustained. Her vocabulary was superior and she read better literature, showing spotty and superficial interest in "cultural" topics. She had a good sense of humor and was somewhat charming in a psychopathic way.

On the Wechsler Adult Intelligence Scale she achieved a Verbal IQ of 99, a Performance IQ of 101, and a Full Scale IQ of 98; all average. Helen went to the twelfth grade in high school, but did not graduate. She was untrained to do most jobs and, the year before she joined the Women's Army Corps, she held nine different jobs.

The summary of the neuropsychodiagnostic evaluation revealed a confused, hypermanic, complicated agitation. Her drawing of her house consisted of two houses within a house, with a ladder going through the middle, to which she freely associated, "my sister is a social climber and, therefore, the ladder." Parenthetically, there was much sibling rivalry with this sister, her only "successful," that is, adjusted, sibling. Her tree was a barren reproduction, with bricks indicating repairment in the bark, to which she said, "Man planted the tree, man repaired the tree; the tree is a symbol, as the cross is a symbol of religion." Actually, the tree is a symbol of her life, with attempts at repairment which have failed her. The drawing of her first person appeared to be a mummy with the head peering through a coffin, to which she freely associated that this made her think of her mother and that this was the last remembrance she actually had of her mother. To say the least, this was a depressing characterization and it brought tears to her eyes, appropriately.

Asked to draw a member of the opposite sex, she drew quite impulsively in an angered fashion, using purples and blues and somber colors, and drew several profiles "of the men in my life." Her Rorschach consisted of many bizarre, negativistic, confusing, emotionally impulsive responses. Her intelligence level was only average. Her mirror-drawing performance was impulsively executed, showing an inability for planning and an inability to handle anxiety generated by this procedure.

In summary, she was a woman who actually measured only average intelligence, but it was apparent that she had at least bright, if not superior, ability, as judged by her sense of humor, sensitivity, vocabulary, and diction. She was also well read and informed about historical and current events. The findings suggested a negativistic, impulsive, uncontrollable, angry, hostile type of individual.

At the staff conference to decide whether or not to recommend lobotomy, this examiner was one to vote against the operation!

Helen was considered a suitable candidate for the unilateral prefrontal lobotomy because other attempts at psychotherapy and medication all failed; these ranged from deep-relationship therapy to electric shock. The night before her operation, Helen was still being evaluated neuropsychodiagnostically, and confessed to this examiner, "I feel like a guinea pig about to get a cerebral castration."

The neurosurgery was unremarkable, and Helen was sent home after a few weeks. The plan was to re-evaluate her psychiatrically and neuropsychodiagnostically once again, with many of the same procedures but with different forms, in order to keep the practice effects to a minimum.

Approximately one month after her operation, Helen appeared for the evaluations and my report was submitted. Not only did she say she was not as angry with herself or other people, but the test results suggested a more complacent attitude and a greater willingness to accept; and agreeableness which was entirely out of character for her.

Her drawing of her house was an uncomplicated structure. Her drawing of a tree was a healthier-looking production. Her female person was a profile of an angelic, cherubic sort, not unlike the patient's own profile. The male drawing was just of a head. The Rorschach, this time, contained fewer responses and were more matter-of-fact and less embellished, without the bizarreness previously elicited; there was less conflict and tension in the content of her Rorschach, also. Her mirror drawing, indeed, was executed with a minimum of anxiety and a maximum of planning. There was less id and erotic preoccupation and less impulsivity. Helen appeared to be more mature and restrained in her ideation and displayed better control.

One year later, Helen was admitted once again, and the neurosurgical team decided to the same prefrontal lobotomy on the other hemisphere. Consequently, the patient was evaluated once again and my report follows.

The patient's Rorschach was quite similar to the first preoperative Rorschach. He drawings were typical for a manic, impulsive person. Her drawing of a house was even more bizarre, with many colors and looking not unlike a sphinx. More id material and more emotion was apparent in this production. Her tree was executed with many colors and was not a healthy tree at all. Her female drawing fell in line with the above productions, and had certain of the bizarre qualities of the first pre-op drawing. A little stick figure was also included, with outstretched hands, to which she commented, "That is me." Again, she stated that the whole production was a drawing of her mother. Much emotionality was expressed in these drawings. A thespian profile, much like John Barrymore doing "Hamlet," with vivid colors was executed. All in all, Helen displayed an impulsive, emotional, hostile personality prior to the second operation, much like the one she possessed prior to the first lobotomy.

Three weeks later, she was up and about in her room, and I repeated many of the same neuropsychological procedures and reported the following: The productions revealed less emotional and more subdued responses. Her total Rorschach responses were down from an original seventy-four to twenty-eight. Her drawing of a man was now a drawing of a ten-year-old. The patient appeared somewhat apathetic and had less initiative, and her drive was diminished considerably. She appeared manageable and cooperative and could be handled more easily, but gone was her spirit and her vitality.

Indeed, she was docile and submissive in a fashion never encountered before. She was uncharacteristically cooperative and clinging. Two months later, we obtained a report on Helen from the veterans' hospital, where she was evaluated by another team: "Patient is a different person. She is now quiet, agreeable and cooperative. She complies with the routine on the ward. She is anxious to mingle with the better patients and participates in recreational activities. She has no appearance of aggression or depression as she used to. She is completely overwhelmed at having to make a decision or to use her judgment, but accepts this, since she is conscious of her inadequacies. Patient is not erotic with either men or women and she is not overly affectionate. However, she has shown an agreeable likeness for some of the other patients. She is apathetic now, has no initiative, cannot solve problems, but seems cheerful and does not want to run away as previously."

THE CATALYST

Several months later, she was discharged from the veterans' hospital. She visited the staff at the hospital and made it a point to see me. She was dressed appropriately and her hair had grown in to show her full head of red hair. She had gotten thinner and appeared svelte. She looked calmer; almost like an automaton with flattened affect and little mood. Her sense of humor was gone and she volunteered little conversation, as though she feared she would say something that might be embarrassing. Helen was a different person, but I am not sure she was a better one. To be sure, she was not sick now, and possibly was out of pain and not suffering. Her charm, energy, and fervor were gone. She was truly a case of "cerebral castration."

IF AT FIRST
YOU DON'T SUCCEED...

In this chapter we shall consider the several underachieving students, clients, and patients I had the privilege of "turning around" toward accomplishments in English Literature, Education, Sociology, Ecology, Psychology, and Medicine. Several went further and obtained their doctorates.

Graduate students were referred at a time when they were unable to complete their dissertations or when they were unable to begin the task of writing. Some had completed all the necessary research, but could not put pen to paper and start the actual writing of their dissertations. Several others became so anxious and nervous merely contemplating the actual research that they developed emotional blocks that prevented progress.

In preparation for the impending therapeutic intervention, even before psychodiagnostic evaluation, I voiced my axiom: "Underachievers are not born, they are made!" I would then put forward my dynamic theory of the process of how one becomes an underachiever with a regimen of how the process may be reversed. I would then impart my message that there is hope and that a method is available to help them achieve once gain. Then and only then, could they be started toward accomplishment scholastically and personally.

While we know that success seems to lead to more success, the converse realization is also true; failure often begets failure. That we are all underachievers, more or less, may comfort some, or that each of us lives in the shadow of underachievement, still, we can start to achieve more. It was in this spirit of accomplishment that I had the privilege of working with several clients and patients who were referred to me by several career and guidance agencies and university mental health departments.

Roy had been raised in an upstate New York community where he excelled in the local high school, but when he came to one of New York City's finest universities, he floundered academically and socially. He had a florid psychiatric nervous breakdown, and was diagnosed as a borderline schizophrenic and told to withdraw from college for a year. He found his way to an agency and was referred to me for follow-up counseling. Roy kept his appointments and preferred to lie down on the couch, even though he knew he was not in orthodox psychoanalytic psychotherapy, even though our approach was psychodynamically oriented psychotherapy, which he preferred. Roy was "all business" as a student and as a patient. He was gifted intellectually, exceedingly well read in literature, history, religion, and Freudian psychoanalysis. Unfortunately, he was disdainful of his parents' middle-class values and lowly educational accomplishments.

In therapy, Roy was obsessional, depressed, and suspicious. After many months of constant talking, almost without letup, he ceased being depressed and suspicious. He began to plan his return to college and he was encouraged to allow his parents to visit him once again, as they had not seen him for almost the year he was in therapy. This had been his choice, to which I also subscribed. After his parents visited him and consulted with me, they were reassured that Roy's prognosis was favorable and he would return to college.

His return to college was unremarkable, except that, after his first semester, he achieved two As and three Bs. Roy was well on his way to becoming an achieving student. He joined several extracurricular activities such as debating society and Hillel. Therapy progressed also, and he was encouraged to date young women at a neighboring college. He made many friends among his own sex, also, and began to demonstrate an interest in liturgical cantorial Hebrew music.

In his last year, Roy made dean's list, much to his parents' pride. We always knew he had it in him and were more blase about this accomplishment. We were also pleased when he applied to the Peace Corps and was accepted to work in Ethiopia. This latter was no simple decision, as Roy had ventured out of the country only to visit Israel during two summers to work at a kibbutz. He signed on to work with the Peace Corps for a two-year term right after graduating from college. When the time arrived for him to leave for Ethiopia, Roy was in the best mental health he had ever been and had achieved a degree of success he had never expected, both personally and academically.

The Peace Corps, in general, and Ethiopia, in particular, had a synergistic beneficial effect on Roy wherein he contributed immeasurably and learned about his religion from the tribe of Judah. When he wrote to me, he informed me that, upon his return, he would pursue a career as a cantor in preparation for the rabbinate at the Jewish Theological Seminary in New York City. Every few years, Roy phones me to tell me of his "supreme happiness in serving his people" and how he owes this all to therapy. I simply say, it was so ordained!

*

A twenty-eight-year-old husband was referred to me by his twenty-six-year-old wife because "he loafed around the house, smoked pot, was lazy, and would not sit down to write his doctoral dissertation."

Fortunately, Jay did not object to consulting with me when his wife made the initial appointment. When he appeared, it was soon apparent to me that he was "stoned," and he admitted he had to have his daily pot. This was a difficult session, as he almost fell asleep on two occasions. He laughed superciliously and spoke very little and replied to my questions with one or two words.

What did emerge from this first interview was that he was still in good standing in the doctoral program at Northwestern University in the Biology Department and, more specifically, in Ecology. Most of his data was in the mainframe computer on the campus at Evanston, and he would have to arrange to spend several days during the summer adding data that he was to accumulate from wetlands in Connecticut where he was studying moss colonies. While living in Greenwich, Joan, his wife, was working in a curtain store as an interior designer and supporting the two of them. He was unemployed and disengaged.

After three sessions, I insisted that Jay refrain from coming to therapy stoned and told him that he was heading nowhere fast. After a few more academic terms, Northwestern would terminate his matriculation for the doctorate so that he would lose the years of schooling, the money invested, and the money he might have earned in the past six years being gainfully employed at some other endeavor. As if hit over the head with a bat, Jay straightened up and awakened. In subsequent months, Jay visited the Connecticut wetlands and accumulated more than enough data to add to his original study. He was also more attentive to Joan and helped her with her hobby of sculptured glass. She began to show her work in local galleries and actually sold several large pieces for corporate lobbies in Stamford and Bridgeport. Jay helped her transport the raw glass pieces and then the finished sculptures to the galleries and corporate headquarters where they were to be unveiled.

As for Jay, he reduced his intake of pot by more than fifty percent, and I was successful in getting him to begin writing a rough draft of his dissertation. After a few more months of writing, he was ready to return to Northwestern to meet with his doctoral committee and work up his data on the computers there. During the spring, he returned once again to defend his thesis with his final draft of his dissertation, and he was successful in obtaining his Ph.D. He remained in therapy and was off pot completely. In addition, he began to teach Biology and Ecology as an adjunct at two local colleges in Westchester County. He also obtained a part-time position in the county's Environmental Protection Agency. With his good fortune and Joan's recognition as an accomplished sculptor, this young couple were well on their way to happiness and contentment.

Months after, Jay decided he had had enough of therapy. He sent me an abstract of his doctoral dissertation and inscribed in his own hand; "...without you, this would never have come to pass; we thank you for everything you have done for us."

THE CATALYST

*

Brenda was a scared, anxious, introverted, underfed twenty-seven-year-old who had been abusing drugs. She was part of a cult group of hippies living in the East Village of New York City. Coming for therapy was a profound decision for her to make, since it would mean "being drummed out of the cult" if she was successful in extricating herself.

Therapy was easy for Brenda to accept, as she had planned to obtain counseling as early as her elementary school days in Fall River, Massachusetts. Her parents were not getting on with one another, and the children were not doing well in school and were being characterized as low achievers. For several months, the family was in family counseling. However, her father found a way to sabotage this effort and none of the family members returned. Brenda did not tell any of her family that she wanted this kind of help, but she put it into her memory bank and, years later, took the initiative herself.

Brenda was very verbal and could free associate easily. Furthermore, she was very facile with vocabulary, so she spoke with ease and almost continuously during entire sessions. She gleaned much insight from my formulations about her sense of inferiority, and began to realize that she had considerable intelligence which she began to tap. This new sense of accomplishment at school and at work bolstered her sense of identity so that she was able to sustain her new-found freedom from rebellious acting-out behavior. Self-confidence and a sense of accomplishment were attitudes she had never experienced before, and these led to successes.

While she was never really "busted," arrested, that is, she was fearful of the track marks left on her arms and being found out that she had a history of heroin. Consequently, she avoided jobs where she would have to give her resume or where she would have to have a physical examination. She had another year of college to obtain a bachelors degree.

A few weeks after getting into therapy, she was able to move into her own walk-up apartment on the upper East Side, get a job as a waitress where the tips were good, and enroll at Hunter to complete her degree. After she graduated with a major in English, she was encouraged to seek employment as a legal secretary, where she felt her salary was astronomical. She was free of all drugs and free from her old hippie friends. She threw herself into modern dance, dieting, and reading the classics. She attended her therapy sessions with fervor and was beginning to achieve physical and mental health. She had no difficulty making new friends and came out of her introverted shell, glowing and radiant. She outgrew her job and re-worked her resume so that she could qualify and obtain an exceedingly rewarding position as an administrative assistant to the chairman and professor of a prestigious hospital and medical school in upper Manhattan. While she feared that her secret would be found out, it never was and she flourished and excelled.

THE CATALYST

Brenda had achieved so much self-confidence and self-worth that she was able to accept my suggestion that she acquire more education and perhaps got for a masters degree in English. This she did at Hunter College, and she did so well that, since she was on a roll, she even contemplated going for a doctorate. She matriculated at Columbia University for the doctorate in English literature, and lost herself in the English and American classics. She read voraciously and could devour several books a week, hold down a taxing position at the hospital, and find the time for modern dance, Weight Watchers, and therapy.

She was ready for her comprehensive exams at Columbia but, for reasons beyond our comprehension, she was not accepted. In past years, this disappointment would have been cause for "shooting up," but now she took it in stride, shed a few tears, thumbed her nose at the high and mighty, and prepared to study at New York University. Her scholarship was outstanding and her grades were exemplary. Her papers were tomes and worthy of publication. While doing well at graduate school, she continued to perform with distinction at her career at the hospital and was earning more and more, with a bonus each year.

A few years after attending New York University, Brenda defended her dissertation successfully and earned her doctorate. Today, she still enjoys her position as administrative assistant but is also writing for publication and teaching Creative Writing and English Literature as an adjunct professor at a local community college.

She still attends to her therapy once a week currently, and also looks forward to her many avocational interests, such as acting, dancing lessons, teaching, and reading modern American literature and the classics.

*

A teaching fellow in the philosophy department of Columbia University consulted me for anxiety associated with his inability to complete his dissertation for the doctorate.

Henry was tense and intense and looked every inch the professor he aspired to become. It was early in January, and this was the last academic year he had before forfeiting all the study and credits he had amassed for his degree, as Columbia had a ten-year limit on procrastination.

In the course of therapy, he spoke freely about his parents' divorce and its effects upon his early schooling and the ensuing psychic depression. This was the most difficult period of his life, as he revered his father and wanted to live with him rather than his mother, whom he saw as a "scatter-brained incompetent." Besides, his father was an accomplished foreign actor and led a bohemian lifestyle which Henry found attractive. Even as a teenager, however, he realized that his father would instill irresponsible attitudes toward scholarship and the work ethic, and life with his mother would be more beneficial in the long run.

THE CATALYST

Henry found himself in a position of raising himself and his mother, as she was "beautiful, but dumb, and inept at bringing me up." He threw himself into his studies and read a book a week in elementary and secondary school, and won a scholarship to Columbia, where he earned a 4.0 grade point average and made Phi Beta Kappa. He did very well on his comprehensive exams and was readily accepted in the doctoral program in Philosophy at Columbia. He moved along quickly and had no trouble achieving As in most of his courses.

After completing all of the course and language requirements without any difficulty at all, and after selecting a topic for his dissertation, he had experienced no anxiety whatsoever. Nonetheless, semester after semester, he put off the actual writing of the dissertation. On several occasions, his committee members and the dean inquired of Henry why there was a delay.

He had completed much of his research on Max Weber, the father of the Protestant work ethic, and obtained approval from his committee to go forward and start the actual writing of his dissertation. This, he could not or would not do at the time.

In therapy, several issues began to emerge. Henry had recently married a doctoral student in Film at New York University, who was busily engaged at writing her dissertation with much dispatch and speed. Her success both on her job and at graduate school had an unusual effect on Henry. He could not deal with the competitive issue, nor with the fact that nothing could stand in her way to forge ahead, even though he had started four years earlier. In therapy, he revealed that he never did well with competition, even though he never had to. However, in marriage, he never thought he would be competing academically to see who got the doctorate first.

We began to talk about his feelings regarding women, and he was never impressed with their intellect. Generalization in a   philosopher was "verboten" professionally, as well as personally, and when he was able to realize this and accept it, he ceased his competitiveness and could admire his wife's diligence and perspicacity. Now he could identify with her scholarship and work ethic.

Rather than being overwhelmed with the task of actually writing the dissertation, we emphasized merely writing one hour before noon and one hour in the afternoon. We did this again during the third week. When the fourth week arrived, Henry volunteered to write for longer periods of time. Before long, he had quite a document in first draft.

When spring came, Henry had most of the dissertation written, which he was able to show to the chairman of the committee. After the Easter recess, the dissertation had been written and was now in the hands of each of the committee members for their reactions. Several changes had to be made but, by and large, it had been accepted, so all that remained was the final typing and copies for the final student defense.

THE CATALYST

During early May, Henry defended successfully, just before the ten-year limit expired, and his doctorate was awarded in June. Meanwhile, his wife obtained her doctorate in Film the following year. They both continued to teach as adjuncts in different departments of different universities. With the ordeal of the dissertation behind him, Henry was able to concentrate now at being relaxed, secure, and attentive to his wife's needs. Their relationship flourished and he "felt warm and alive for the first time in my life." In December, both had been offered academic posts at the same university in a large midwestern urban center. Henry has kept in touch, is writing a text, and has conquered procrastination.

*

Francois had a life story worthy of a Victor Hugo hero. Although born to a Jewish family, he was raised by Catholic nuns in Belgium during the Nazi occupation. His parents had been gassed at Auschwitz, but he made his way to safety with Christian pilgrims going from Germany to France and onward to Belgium. This trek occurred before his eighth year.

He remained in Europe until he was sixteen and then surfaced to a Jewish refugee agency and found himself in New York City on the lower East Side. To support himself, he worked as a photographer's assistant in New York's garment district. He was underpaid and decided to freelance to supplement his meager stipend.

One rich client he had possessed an invaluable collection of Judaica artifacts, jewelry, rare books,and paintings. Francois was hired to photograph this entire collection, piece by piece. Being passive and diffident, the young man never asked for his agreed-upon fee and, consequently, this came up in therapy, session after session. Being low in funds practically meant starvation and impending removal from his modest flat. After several weeks, I felt I had had enough and decided to phone this rich collector for my patient, as it was readily apparent to both of us that he would not or could not ask for his fee himself. I did this with Francois sitting in front of me.

I introduced myself to this man, mentioned that Francois was with me, and I wondered whether he had forgotten about the small fee owed Francois. To be sure, he knew he owed him some money, but just how much, Francois had never told him. Indeed, he would write a check immediately to the young man just as soon as he informed him. However, the collector was incredulous to think that a therapist would take such an interest and actually phone himself inquiring about such a matter. I pointed out that this young man's obsequiousness has been in his way most of his life and, if he was to progress toward maturity, he would have to learn how to remedy this fault. And perhaps with his help and mine, we elders could help Francois achieve his goal. "I have been in psychoanalysis and therapy for decades but never did I hear of a therapist taking such a position and actually doing what you have done by phoning me in behalf of a patient; I would like to meet you and buy you a drink."

Arrangements were made for Francois to pick up his check, which was considerably more than he expected. This event had a salutary effect on him, and he made rapid strides toward independence and self-worth.

Some weeks later, I heard from the art collector, who invited me to have a drink, and a mutually agreeable time was arranged and we met. It soon developed that we had much in common in the art world and socially among other collectors, artists, therapists, and publishers. Indeed, many Saturday afternoons were spent visiting art galleries, artists' ateliers, and museums. Thanks to our friendship, I, too, have become a collector of contemporary art. My love of classical music was useful in contributing to his cultural interests and we have attended many concerts, ballet performances, and theatrical productions together. We have been friends for the past twenty-five years.

Francois, in the meantime, began to flourish emotionally and continued in therapy toward greater maturity. Photography as a career was re-explored, and we began to look into other choices that would be less sporadic with a steady paycheck. I encouraged him to consider returning to college to complete his degree and take educational courses and work towards teaching as a career. In addition, he was fluent in German and French and spoke English with a charming accent, so he could either teach in the city school system or in some private school. Photography could become an avocation.

Francois enrolled in a local city college program in the evening and began to take his education seriously, working during the day as an assistant to a fashion photographer. After four semesters, he was awarded a degree with an Education major in languages. He had no trouble getting a position in a prestigious private school in the city and he earned extra pay for teaching photography to the senior classes, as well as teaching French and German.

The passivity which had permeated Francois' psyche when he entered therapy all but vanished when economic and professional security was achieved. Socially, he flourished as well, and he met and befriended men and women among his colleagues. He was an excellent teacher, full of compassion and empathy. As a matter of fact, all of his projects were permeated with zeal and passion. He was loved by his students, parents, and colleagues. Francois moved up the academic ladder and obtained a masters degree in Romance Languages, which contributed further to his professional career and was emotionally rewarding, as well.

*

A brilliant doctoral student in Sociology was referred to me by the graduate center of a neighboring university. This young man had completed all of his course work but was mired down in the writing of his dissertation.

THE CATALYST

He had accumulated some of his data, but he needed to work it up statistically and put pen to paper and commence with the actual writing. Years had passed and he was not progressing. All sorts of events and personal crises intervened to obstruct the completion of his dissertation.

Joe was the only child of Holocaust survivors. His father had a clinical manic-depressive, depressive disorder and was under the care of the Veterans Administration's Psychiatric Department for more than thirty years; he had been a veteran of World War II and his illness was controlled by medication. His mother not only raised Joe, practically all alone, but she had worked as a legal secretary for more than twenty-five years and nursed her husband through episodic hospitalizations. She truly was a survivor and still is. From her example, Joe drew self-discipline, drive, love of hard work, persistence, and perseverance. From his father's behavior, he learned to avoid succumbing to illness and irresponsibility.

During a weak moment in the latter part of his adolescence, Joe married a young, needy, unstable woman, equally neurotic. This marriage replicated his parents'; he assumed his mother's role of caregiver and his wife was to play out his father's role. All of this soon became apparent to him in the course of therapy, and he realized that his preoccupation with his wife's needs and fears would make her become dysfunctional and require his close surveillance. Not only was this draining on his emotional equilibrium, but it was time-consuming and actually unrewarding. His concern for his father's welfare and mental health was a compelling force interfering with his scholarship and career. In therapy, we had to reorder his priorities without guilt.

Identifying with his mother taught him to persevere as a scholar and as a teacher. He obtained a post as an adjunct instructor at a suburban state college, but his academic clock was ticking, as it was imperative that he earn his doctorate before the deadline of ten years.

Although it was important that in therapy he discuss intrapsychic pressures and interpersonal conflicts with his wife, her family, his colleagues, and students, it was also necessary to balance his sense of responsibility to his career as well as to these people and his father. Invariably, when he would attempt to start his writing, either his wife would come down with some psychosomatic complaint, or his father would have to be rehospitalized, or his father-in-law would require a trip to his physician for his heart condition. Joe was always on call for some impending emergency, and he would respond.

After a year and a half of this kind of delay, he realized he could not permit these intrusions, and he learned to say no on several occasions. In the fall of one year, after he started his teaching, he announced to me that he would begin to coordinate all of his data, work it up statistically, and begin the introduction to his dissertation. He did most of his writing in the early morning before he left for the suburbs to teach.

THE CATALYST

Luckily, his wife started to teach as a substitute in a New York City elementary school, and she was often out mornings. Once he gathered momentum, Joe's commitment to his doctorate was the major force for the next several months. He sacrificed nothing; no emergency went unanswered. His responsibility to students' needs, wife's needs, parents and in-laws, who were chauffeured from physician and hospital, was available unstintingly. Nonetheless, he made remarkable progress and, before long, he had a rough draft of the first four chapters of his dissertation. Even more significant was the change in his attitude about himself and the self-discipline he had found that enabled him to prioritize the demands thrust upon him.

Joe took control of his academic and career roles and put his personal life in a subordinate position for a while. He discovered that his wife functioned just as well without his close scrutiny and that his elders found other people to drive to physicians. This freed him for more time in the statistical lab before the computer and gave him more time for writing. After a few months of writing and incorporating his data and results in the ensuing chapters, the rough draft was complete.

A sense of self-worth and accomplishment became evident, and Joe displayed a change in attitude toward psychological infirmities. He was no longer fearful of impending nervous breakdowns in his wife and began to regard her as a more competent individual; indeed, she was no longer a substitute teacher, but was promoted to full-time classification with all the ensuing benefits. His father's illness changed in that the periods of wellness were of longer duration than formerly and, as a consequence, there were fewer hospitalizations.

His career began to take off and he completed his dissertation in time to defend his thesis, so his degree was awarded in June. His parents were very proud of his accomplishment; his wife was not impressed. He began sending out resumes to universities, looking for faculty positions, but it took several months before he even had interviews. Fortunately, a fine university on Long Island hired him as both an administrative assistant dean and assistant professor of Sociology.

He performed so well at both tasks that he was beginning to distinguish himself as a brilliant strategist between faculty and students. Professionally, Joe could not have done better. Personally, Joe could not have done worse. By this time, he and his wife were living apart and he was waiting for her to divorce him. Physically, the marriage had been over years before; emotionally, he felt married in terms of his responsibility toward her.

For the next several years, his therapy was concerned with his wife's moves toward divorce and how he would react to this event and his writings that could lead to tenure at the university. Tenure occurred first and, months later, his wife instituted a   divorce action which was uncontested. Joe finally came into his own, and he wore his new-found freedom as though he had earned it the hard way. He preferred full-time teaching and some administrative work that went along with being the chair of his department, and ceased being a dean. He published a book and was busy at work on three other volumes with colleagues. He was building an international reputation in his field and he was presenting papers throughout the U.S. and abroad. His mother had retired, so she had more time to look after his father. Joe was in healthy control of his destiny and he enjoyed the sensation of success.

*

A young man of seventeen who had just graduated from a special music and art high school, part of the New York City educational system, was referred to me by his guidance counselor for severe depression. He had excelled in music, and the piano was his instrument. I had never heard him play but, early in therapy, he announced that he had never cared for music but that it was to please his mother that he had ever accepted lessons in the first place.

His father was a passive, incompetent worker who could never hold on to a job for more than one year. Indeed, after months of relating stories about his father in terms of ineptness around the house and in the family automobile, it soon became clear that his father could have had an organic brain syndrome disorder. However, I was in no position to render a diagnosis; I merely had the thought and I filed it away.

In my work with Steve, I listened to many of his remarks about his parents' incompatibility and father's physical abuse and destructive behavior. Uncontrollable rage and unabashed violence exploded without reason frequently. Steve could not inform his parents that he preferred to major in sciences rather than music, and that he would teach science rather than music. They demonstrated no real interest in which college he went to, just as long as they would not have to pay for his education. Thus, he enrolled in City College of the City University of New York system, and obtained a part-time job in the work-study program. He was encouraged to study away from his noisy, tumultuous, strife-torn home and use the library facilities of his college and local libraries in midtown Manhattan.

Steve was learning how to study and becoming a scholar. His grades for the first two years were outstanding, with eight As and two Bs. He joined the pre-med society and listened to invited speakers from neighboring hospitals and medical schools. I arranged for him to volunteer at the Presbyterian Hospital-Columbia University, College of Physicians and Surgeons, and he continued with the work-study program at the college.

Steve epitomized the adage, "If you want something done, ask a busy person to do it." He used his home as a hotel; he slept, ate, and showered there; very little else. He would see his mother on occasion, but his father, rarely. He missed his mother, but she understood what he was up to and, on several occasions, she would come in to see me just to keep up with his progress. Steve was maturing at a rapid pace and he was planning a life after college. He was still doing exemplary work in his subjects and his grade point average was close to 3.85; he had made the dean's list by his fourth year.

He continued to volunteer at the hospital, and I arranged to get him into a lab where he could see some of the high-tech procedures in operation. Furthermore, he was allowed to use the medical libraries of Columbia University, College of Physicians & Surgeons with his plastic ID.

One evening, his mother called him at the hospital and summoned him home. His father had suddenly gotten ill, was vomiting and complaining of a severe headache, and was unable to stand upright. Steve told her to call his physician and said he would be right home. By the time he arrived, his father had passed away, and the next day they learned, via autopsy, that the man had a glioblastoma; a brain tumor.

Therapy for the next several months dealt with Steve's guilt about his treatment of his father and his unwillingness to be tolerant "of the man's disabilities and complaints, which may have been precursors of his eventual brain tumor." This sounded more like a neurologist's report than a son talking about his recently deceased father.

I had heard of a part-time position available at the Presbyterian Hospital, and suggested that Steve follow up this lead. He did, and was chosen to work in a lab during the summer and, upon graduation, he was to work full-time. I also suggested that he take the MCAT (tests for med school).

He learned a lot and must have contributed much, also, as he earned a stunning recommendation from the professor he worked for when he applied to Columbia University, College of Physicians and Surgeons. Months later, he heard that he had been accepted.

Now well on his way to a career in medicine, Steve really had no time for therapy; nor was there the emergency that he felt originally. We agreed that he could call at any time and we would meet. After he graduated from Physicians and Surgeons, he obtained a residency in ophthalmology and spent five years becoming a specialist. Some years ago, he came to see me to inform me that he owed so much to me and that he was going to California to teach and practice and do surgery. A while later, I received newspaper clips of the remarkable laser surgery he was doing on the eyes of infants. He was operating under a high-powered microscope in a space on the eye one millimeter by six millimeters, in infants a few weeks old. He was distinguishing himself so well that he had a lab of his own and several operating rooms where he was in charge of the residency program and teaching specialists from all over the world.

*

THE CATALYST

"If at first you don't succeed, try, try again." This adage has not been expressed for decades, and yet there are some of us from another generation who were raised on it. The underachievers chronicled in this chapter all had in common many of the following characteristics:

1) Negative self-concept with unconscious acting out;
2) Negative evaluations of others;
3) Pessimistic outlooks;
4) Excessive hostility;
5) Low levels of frustration tolerance;
6) Anomie, were loners, were withdrawn;
7) Escaped from, rather than attempted to, resolve frustration;
8) Feelings of inferiority and lack of confidence;
9) Rationalization of their errors;
10) Refusal to accept responsibility for poor grades;
11) Immaturity, "Wanting what they wanted when they wanted it";
12) Lack of self-discipline;
13) Inability to work for distant goals;
14) Less planful, believing in luck, fate, and external breaks;
15) Socially overextended with extracurricular out-of-school activities;
16) From culturally and educationally deprived homes;
17) Had parents who were negative toward education and scholastic achievement;
18) Lack of communication with parents;
19) Permissive parents who made few demands;
20) Poor study habits;
21) Displaced hostility to parents;
22) Ineffectual father and dominant, effective mother;
23) Inability to focus, concentrate, and get started;
24) Labeled "underachiever" early in school; and
25) Restlessness related to habitual television viewing and unstructured habits of hedonism.

As our nation is in a race for survival and our children are one of our treasured resources, we must do all that is in our power to harness accomplishment and achievement. This task can be done via a clear understanding of the psychodynamics of academic underachievement in the first place, and then adopting a positive remedial attitude. Underachieving children will usually grow up to be underachieving adults unless some sort of therapeutic intervention is introduced. This could be counseling, guidance, or psychotherapy.

Assuming that none of these is available, recommended, or sought, then we can expect a diminished self-concept, lack of confidence, and a discouraged, confused adolescent with low self-esteem. Negativism, avoidance, self-recrimination, and loss of self-respect is associated with a decade of dropping out, depression, and possible abuse of drugs. A weakened ego-ideal and a poor concept of self is associated with an unconscious need to fail, through diminished motivation with the usual secondary gains of incipient neuroses in a dysfunctional adult.

Thus, the issue is not one of intellectual inadequacy but is due to faulty learning skills. Failure is thus associated with the entire learning-school process. The conditioning reinforced in learning specific subjects is generalized to all school situations. A state of panic is then related to everything educational and worth learning. What follows is the inevitable, negative self-fulfilling prophecy!

Failure begets failure. Anxiety pervades thinking and obstructs judgment. Fear can diminish ability to concentrate, causing avoidance, apathy, constricted goals, bewilderment, ego constriction, and, frequently, substitution of unhealthy momentary satisfactions in the form of drug abuse. The complainer now begins to project his own handicaps on others; it's never "my fault." This confirms Disraeli's statement that, "It is much easier to be critical than correct." Unfortunately, such persons are willing to accept the fact that they are functioning at a much-reduced level rather than doing something positive to remedy their situation.

Underachievers come in all varieties of human kind and in many settings—in schools, colleges, graduate and professional centers, in the workplace, in the professions, courts, civil servants, politics, management, labor unions, congress, religious leaders, and media personnel. Wherever persons are not living up to their intellectual potential and possess untreated subject disabilities with feelings of stupidity, demoralization, and poor motivation toward knowledge and education, we have the seeds of neuroses. Included among the symptoms and syndromes are: tension, depression, neurasthenic fatigue, somatization of anxiety into headaches, gastrointestinal complaints, restlessness, lack of confidence, indecision, phobias, sleeplessness, and irritability. An overwhelming sense of frustration in concert with homeostatic disharmony produces a cacophony of ego dysfunction with excuses and neurotic self-destructive behaviors.

Persons in crises sometimes attempt to heal themselves by self-medication nostrums such as alcohol and other drugs. Others seek more professional help. With effective procedures in the hands of professionals, true potentials can be determined, areas of impairment assayed, assets, as well as liabilities, uncovered, and steps to remove discovered disabilities can be recommended. These productive rehabilitative remedies remove the threat of future failure. They set off the first chain reaction toward success. Knowing and sensing this is encouraging to the re-emerging, healthy ego, which enhances further therapeutic experiences. At this point, I usually assure the client or the patient, which ever appellation he prefers, that, "I am not a shrink—rather, I am an ego dilator." I convince them that they have done their own shrinking of their ego; I will try to help them expand it!

As therapy proceeds, the patient experiences a feeling of success which is almost self-sustaining. The narrowed, constricted *Weltanschauung* allows for an initial, continuous source of satisfaction. This is commensurate with limited potentials at even lower energy levels than before, but it ensures success rather than failure. Thus, a new taste of competence permeates the psychic diet rather than the onerous odor of constant failure. Diminished anxiety and a desensitization toward work enables energy, heretofore wasted in disorganized activities and worry, to be used constructively. More such experiences geared toward successes contributes to a positive self-fulfilling prophecy!

EPILOGUE

After I delivered a paper on underachievement, the following editorial appeared in *The Voice,* "A Report on News of American Reform Judaism."

"American-Jewish parents have been criticized for being over-permissive with their children. They have been conspicuous in the ranks of those advocating 'progressive education.'

"It was not always so. This is a code of education drawn up by the leaders of the Jewish community in twelfth-century England:

> 'From month to month, you shall increase my son's task. If this month he can learn half the weekly portion of Scripture, next month he must go through the whole. From Tammus (June‡July) to Tishri he must go through the weekly portion in Hebrew, and from Tishri to Nisan in the vernacular. Then the boy is six years old. In his seventh year he must learn the Aramaic version from the book and not by heart and translate it into the vulgar tongue. In his eighth and ninth year he must take the prophets and Hagiographa.'

"Our sages say further: At ten years to the Mishna. Then the lad is to be introduced to the Talmud, at first in the Tractate Beracoth (or Benedictions) and the smaller tractates which belong to the order Moed (Festivals).

> 'The teachers shall instruct the lads to translate the Aramaic version (Targum) of the Scripture into the vernacular, so that they be practised in the language of the Talmud (Aramaic) and can be easily introduced to the study of Halacha (Rabinic Law)..."When the overseer notices one of the lads to be of slow intellect, he shall lead him to his father and say to him, 'God grant thy son power to do noble deeds, but for the study of the Law he is too slow of intellect.' Otherwise, the talented boys would be kept back by the more backward ones...'

"Very much to the same point is a recent theory spawned by psychologist Dr. Arthur Weider. His claim is that children become 'underachievers' in school because of 'unconscious or partly conscious feelings' towards their parents. Those who are 'unwilling or unable to oppose their parents directly through argument or disobedience find academic failure an excellent means of expressing their suppressed rebellion.' He advocates sub-theories in support of the major theme. Among them is one that states that where 'mother is interested in learning and father is not—the son interprets learning as a feminine trait, and rejects it.'

"When we contrast the two statements above, we get the uneasy feeling that, in certain areas, we have been going downhill since the twelfth century."

REFERENCES

7.   Warren, H. C., & Carmichael, L. (1930) *Elements of Human Psychology.*
      Boston: Houghton Mifflin Co.

8.   *Minnesota Paper Form Board Test.* (1939) New York:
      The Psychological Corporation.

14.   Benton, A. Weider, A., & Blauvelt, J. (1941) Performances of Adult
      Patients on the Bellevue Intelligence Scales and the Revised
      Stanford-Binet. *Psychiatric Quarterly,* 15:4, 802–806.

16.   Weider, A. (1943) Effects of Age on the Bellevue Intelligence Scales
      in Schizophrenic Patients. *Psychiatric Quarterly,* 17:2, 337–346.

18.   Weider, A., Mittelmann, B., Wechsler, D., & Wolff, H. G., (Jan. 22, 1944)
      The Cornell Selectee Index: A Method for Quick Testing of Selec-
      tees for the Armed Forces, *Journal of the American Medical
      Association,* 124: 224–228.

      Vonachen, H. A., Mittelmann, B., Kronenberg, M. H., Weider, A.,
      Brodman, K., & Wolff, H. G., (1946) A Comprehensive Mental
      Hygiene Program at Caterpillar Tractor Co.: Improving Human
      Relationships in Industry, *Industrial Medicine,* 15: 179–184.

      Mittelmann, B., Weider, A., Vonachen, H. A., Kronenberg, M. H.,
      Weider, N., Brodman, K., & Wolff, H. G., (1945) Detection and
      Management of Personality and Psychosomatic Disorders Among
      Industrial Personnel. *Psychosomatic Medicine,* 7: 359–367.

      Weider, A., & Mittelmann, B. (1946) Personality and Psychosomatic
      Disturbances Among Industrial Personnel. *American Journal
      of Orthopsychiatry,* 16:4, 631–639.

      Weider, A., Levi, J., & Risch, F. (1943) Performances of Problem
      Children on the Bellevue Intelligence Scales and the Revised Stan-
      ford-Binet. *Psychiatric Quarterly,* 17:4, 695–701.

      Weider, A., Mittelmann, B., Wechsler, D., & Wolff, H. G. (1943)
      The Cornell Selectee Index: A Method for Quick Testing of

Selectees for the Armed Forces, *Transactions of the American Neurological Association,* 126–129.

Weider, A., Mittelmann, B., Wechsler, D., & Wolff, H. G., (1944) The Cornell Selectee Index: Short Form to be Used at Induction, at Reception and During Hospitalization. *War Psychiatry,* 29–32.

Weider, A., Mittelmann, B., Wechsler, D., & Wolff, H. G., (1944) The Cornell Service Index: A Method for Quickly Assaying Personality and Psychosomatic Disturbances in Men in the Armed Forces. *Transactions of the American Neurological Association,* 92–95.

Weider, A., & Mittelmann, B., (1945) Personality and Psychosomatic Disturbances in Patients on Medicine and Surgical Wards: A Survey of 450 Admissions, *Psychosomatic Medicine,* 7:4.

19.   Weider, A., (1945) *Screening the Neuropsychiatrically Unfit Selectee From the Armed Forces.* Ph.D. Dissertation, Ann Arbor: University of Michigan Microfilm.

20.   Weider, A., (1945) The Emotionally Disturbed Veteran Returns to Industry. *National Safety Council Annual Newsletter.*

Weider, A., & Wechsler, D., (1946) The Cornell Indices and Cornell Word Form: No. 2. Results. *Annals of the New York Academy of Sciences,* 46: 579–587.

Weider, A., & Mittelmann, B., (1947) The Incidence of Personality Disturbance and Their Relation to Age, Rank, and Duration of Hospitalization in Patients with Medical and Surgical Disorders in a Military Hospital. *Psychosomatic Medicine,* 9:6.

Weider, A., (1947) Mental Hygiene in Industry: A Clinical Psychologist's Contribution. *Journal of Clinical Psychology,* 3:4.

Weider, A., (1947) Psychiatric and Psychological Procedures in Job Placement. Abstract of an address given before and published in the *36th National Safety Congress Transactions,* Vol. II.

Weider, A., Mittelmann, B., Wechsler, D., & Wolff, H. G. (1946) The Cornell Index: A Method for Quickly Assaying Personality and Psychosomatic Disturbances To Be Used As An Adjunct To Interview. *Psychosomatic Medicine,* 8:6.

Weider, A., & Mittelmann, B., (1947) The Relation of Personality Disturbances to Duration of Convalescence From Acute Respiratory Infections. *Psychosomatic Medicine,* 9:1.

Weider, A., Mittelmann, B., Wechsler, D., & Wolff, H. G., (1948) *Cornell Index (Manual),* New York: Psychological Corporation.

Bakwin, R. M., Weider, A., & Bakwin, H., (1948) Mental Testing In Children. *Journal of Pediatrics,* 33:3, 384–394.

Brower, D. & Weider, A., (1950) Projective Techniques in Business and Industry. In L. E. Abt and L. Bellak (eds.), *Projective Psychology,* 437–461, New York: Knopf.

21. Weider, A., & Noller, P. A., (1950) Objective Studies of Children's Drawings of Human Figures: I. Sex Awareness and Socio-Economic Level, *Journal of Clinical Psychology,* 6:4, 319–385.

Weider, A., (1951) Some Aspects of an Industrial Mental Hygiene Program, *Journal of Applied Psychology,* 35:6, 383–385.

Weider, A., Noller, P.A. & Schramm, T. A., (1951) The Wechsler Intelligence Scale for Children and the Revised Stanford-Binet, *Journal of Consulting Psychology,* 15:4, 330–333.

Weider, A., & Noller, P.A., (1953) Objective Studies of Children's Drawings of Human Figures: II. Sex, Age, Intelligence, *Journal of Clinical Psychology,* 9:1, 20–23.

Weider, A., (1953) *Contributions Toward Medical Psychology: Theory and Psychodiagnostic Methods.* New York: The Ronald Press Company, (Vol. I & II).

22. Weider, A., (1977) *Readings In Behavioral Sciences: Expanded Edition.* New York: Dabor Services.

Weider, A., (1977) *Psychodiagnostic Methods for the Behavioral Sciences: Expanded Edition.* New York: Dabor Services.

23. Weider, A., (1954) Methoden Zur Intelligenzprufung nach Wechsler (a chapter in *Handbuch fur Kinisch-Psychollogische Natoden*). Von Dr. Erich Stern (ed.), Zurich: R schar Verlag.

Weider, A., Mittelmann, B., Wechsler, D., & Wolff, H. G. (1955) Further Developments of the Cornell Word Form. *Psychiatric Quarterly,* 29:4, 588–594.

Guthrie, T. C., Berlin, L., Weider, A., Goodell, H., & Wolff, H. G., (1955) Studies in Human Cerebral Function: The Capacity to Terminate an Adaptive Pattern When it is No Longer Appropriate. *Transactions of American Neurological Association,* 70–72.

Guthrie, T. C., & Weider, A., (1955) Studies in Human Cerebral Function: The Capacity for Orientation As Measured by The Minute Estimation Test. *Transactions of American Neurological Association,* 95–97.

Berlin, L., Guthrie, T. C., Weider, A., Goodell, H., & Wolff, H. G., (1955) Studies in Human Cerebral Function: The Effects of Mescaline and Lysergic Acid on Cerebral Processes Pertinent to Creative Activity. *Journal of Nervous and Mental Disease*, 122:5, 487–491.

Weider, A., (1962) *Contribuciones A La Psicologia Medica*, Eudeba: Argentina: Editorial Universitaria De Buenos Aires.

Weider, A., (1967) Underachievement: The Current Crisis in Education. *Counselors Information Service*, 22, #4.

"Low Grades Mirror Rage": Science, October 6, 1967.

Guthrie, T. C., Dunbar, H. S., & Weider, A., (1970) L-Dopa: Effect on Highest Integrative Functions in Parkinsonism. *Transactions of the American Neurological Association*, 95: 250–252.

Weider, A., (July 4, 1971) The Way Our Children Play Can Save Their Mental Health. *Family Weekly*, Page 7.

"Doctor Says Bad Students Spite Parents": *The Washington Post*, August 14, 1967.

Editorial: *The Voice: A Report on News of American Reform Judaism*, September 22, 1968.

24. "You're Really Something": *Christopher News Notes*, #229, February 15, 1969.

25. Anderson, Jack, "The Calley File": *New York Post*, May 23, 1972.

Butler, Ed, "Calley Insane at My Lai, Unused File Says": *The Virginian-Pilot*, May 28, 1972.

27. Weider, A., (1971) Underachievement Revisited: Still the Current Crisis in Education. *Counselors Information Service*, 26, #3.

Weider, A., (1973) The Science Teacher Assays the Underachiever. *The Science Teacher*, 40:1, 19‡21.

Weider, A., (1974) Innovative Counseling Modalities to Span the Generation Gap in the 1970s. *Counselors Information Service*.

Weider, A., "Air Pollution and New York City": An address before Mayor John Lindsay, June 12, 1973.

33. Vecsey, G., "A Dose of Applied Psychology Draws Diners and Feeds an Ego": *The New York Times*, November 27, 1976.

36. Whelton, C., "They Came from New Jersey: UFO Update": *The Village Voice*, October 3, 1977.

42. Thomas, R. M., 'Waiting for Reggie': *The New York Times,* October 20, 1977.

46. Stathos, H. J., "The People's Psychologist Show" Breaks Ground —and Bread. Restaurant is Studio for New Cable Series": *News World,* September 30, 1979.

54. Bush, G. W., "State of the Union Message": *The New York Times,* February 1, 1990.

62. *White House Conference on Children* (1970). Forum 15:350.

63. *Growing Up Drug Free: A Parent's Guide to Prevention.* (1990). Washington, D.C.: U.S. Department of Education.

65. Council of Foundations, (1990) *The Atlantic Monthly: Supplement,* p.7.

66. Buber, M., (1923) *I and Thou,* New York: Macmillan.

69. Schiller, F., (1954) *On the Aesthetic Education of Man.* New Haven: Yale University Press.

74. Yeats, W. B., (1940) *The Second Coming* (The Variorum Edition of Poems, eds. Allt, P. & Alspach, R. K.) New York: Macmillan Publishing Co.

75. Dylan, B., (1968) *Bob Dylan Song Book.* New York: M. Witmark & Sons.

76. Friedenberg, E. Z., (1959) *The Vanishing Adolescent.* New York: Dell Publishing Company.

Reisman, D., (1961) *The Lonely Crowd.* New Haven: Yale University Press.

Ortega Y Gasset, J., (1932) *The Revolt of the Masses.* New York: Norton, W. & W., Co. Inc.

Whyte, W. H., Jr., (1956) *The Organization Man.* New York: Simon & Schuster, Inc.

Fromm, E., (1976) *Man for Himself.* New York: Holt, Rinehart, & Winston, Inc.

Huxley, A., (1959) *Collected Essays of Aldous Huxley.* New York: Harper Row Publishing Inc.

Wylie, P., (1955) *Generation of Vipers.* New York: Holt, Rinehart, & Winston, Inc.

Sartre, J. P., (1958) *No Exit: A Play in One Act.* New York: French, Inc.

Plato, (1945) *Republic.* New York: Oxford University Press.

Lorand, S., & Schneer, H. (ed.) (1961) *Adolescents: Psychoanalytic Approach to Problems and Therapy.* New York: Paul B. Hoeber, Inc.

77. Weider, A., (1971) Underachievement Revisited:
    Still the Current Crisis in Education. *Counselors Information Service,* 26, #3.

    Laing, R., (1967) *The Politics of Experience.* New York: Penguin Books.

    Barr, D., "What Did We Do Wrong?": *The New York Times Magazine.* November 26, 1967, p.36.

80. Toffler, A., "Future Shock". *Playboy Magazine.* Chicago: Hefner, H. M., February 1970.

81. Gioscia V., (1969) LSD Subcultures: Acidoxy versus Orthodoxy. *American Journal of Orthopsychiatry,* 39:13.

    Gioscia, V., (1969) Groovin' on Time: Fragments of a Sociology of the Psychedelic Experience. Madison, Wis., Stashing. *Psychedelic Drugs,* pp 167–176.

    Masters, R. E. L., & Huston, J., (1966) *The Varieties of Psychedelic Experience.* New York: Holt, Rinehart & Winston.

    McLuhan, M., (1966) *Understanding Media: The Extensions of Man.* New York: Signet Books.

83. Shepard, S., (1970) *Operation Sidewinder: A Play in Two Acts.* Indianapolis: Bobbs-Merrill & Company.

85. Lee, F., "Dial-an-Ear: Young People Tell Young People Their Troubles": *The New York Times,* April 30, 1993.

175. Stone, H., "Editorial: *The Voice: A Report on News of American Reform Judaism,* September 22, 1968.

Index